Edward John Routh, Henry William Watson

Cambridge Senate-House Problems and Riders for the Year 1860

With solutions

Edward John Routh, Henry William Watson

Cambridge Senate-House Problems and Riders for the Year 1860
With solutions

ISBN/EAN: 9783337152031

Printed in Europe, USA, Canada, Australia, Japan

Cover: Foto ©Suzi / pixelio.de

More available books at **www.hansebooks.com**

Cambridge
Senate-House Problems and Riders

FOR THE YEAR 1860;

WITH SOLUTIONS.

BY

THE REV. H. W. WATSON, M.A.
LATE FELLOW OF TRINITY COLLEGE.

AND

E. J. ROUTH, M.A.
FELLOW AND ASSISTANT TUTOR OF ST PETER'S COLLEGE, CAMBRIDGE
AND EXAMINER IN THE UNIVERSITY OF LONDON.

Cambridge:
MACMILLAN AND CO.
AND 23, HENRIETTA STREET, COVENT GARDEN,
London.
1860.

Cambridge:
PRINTED BY C. J. CLAY, M.A.
AT THE UNIVERSITY PRESS.

PREFACE.

THE value of a Collection of Solutions depends in great measure on the fact that every Problem is solved by the framer of the question, thus showing the student the manner in which he was expected to proceed in the Senate-House. The Moderators desire therefore to thank the Examiners for the many valuable Solutions of the Problems set by them, by which the book has been made more complete than it would otherwise have been.

The Senior Moderator also acknowledges his obligation to Mr DROOP, Fellow of Trinity College, for much valuable assistance, and particularly for the suggestion and the solution of the three following Problems, viz. No. vi. of Tuesday Morning, Jan. 17, and Nos. 3 and 5 of Wednesday Morning, Jan. 18.

SOLUTIONS OF SENATE-HOUSE PROBLEMS AND RIDERS

FOR THE YEAR EIGHTEEN HUNDRED AND SIXTY.

TUESDAY, *Jan.* 3. 9 *to* 12.

JUNIOR MODERATOR.   Arabic numbers.
SENIOR EXAMINER.   Roman numbers.

1. IF a straight line DME be drawn through the middle point M of the base of a triangle ABC, so as to cut off equal parts AD, AE from the sides AB, AC, produced if necessary, respectively, then shall BD be equal to CE.

Through C draw CF parallel to AB, and cutting DE in F. Then the two triangles DMB, FMC are clearly equal, and therefore $CF = BD$. Again, CF being parallel to AB, the angle CFE = the angle ADE, and because $AD = AE$, the angle ADE = angle AED; whence it easily follows that $CF = CE$.

2. Shew how to construct a rectangle which shall be equal to a given square; (1) when the sum and (2) when the difference of two adjacent sides is given.

The first case is too obvious to require any solution. In the second case, refer to the figure in Euclid, Book II. Prop. 14. A little consideration will shew that GE is twice the difference between the two sides BE, ED. Whence the following construction. Take GE = half the given difference, describe a circle BHF with radius equal to the side of the given square, and cutting GE produced in B and F. Then BE, EF are the sides of the rectangle required.

3. If two chords AB, AC be drawn from any point A of a circle, and be produced to D and E, so that the rectangle AC, AE is equal to the rectangle AB, AD, then if O be the centre of the circle, AO is perpendicular to DE.

Since $AB . AD = AC . AE$, a circle may be described about $BCED$. Therefore the angle $BDE = BCA$. Hence if A and B be fixed while C moves round the circle, the angle ADE will be constant and the locus of E will be a straight line. Take AC to pass through O and cut the circle in C' and DE in P. Then as before the angle $APD = ABC' =$ a right angle.

iv. Describe an isosceles triangle having each of the angles at the base double of the third angle.

If A be the vertex, and BD the base of the constructed triangle, D being one of the points of intersection of the two circles employed in the construction, and E the other, and AE be drawn meeting BD produced in F, prove that FAB is another isosceles triangle of the same kind.

For ADE is an isosceles triangle, and the angle AED at the base is the supplement of the angle ACD in the opposite segment of the circle. Hence $AED = BCD$ and therefore by Euclid $= ABD$, and also the angles ADE, ADB are equal, therefore the third angle $DAE =$ the third angle BAD. Hence the whole angle BAE is double the angle BAD, and therefore equal to ABD. Hence the triangle FAB is isosceles, and each of the angles at the base is equal to the angles at the base of ABD. Therefore, &c.

v. Prove that the straight lines bisecting one angle of a triangle internally and the other two externally pass through the same point.

Let the exterior angles A and C of the triangle ABC be bisected by AD, CO, meeting each other in O; then BO will bisect the angle ABC. Because AD bisects the exterior angle A, $BA : BD :: AC : CD$. And because CO bisects the angle ACD, therefore $AC : CD :: AO : OD$, therefore $BA : BD :: AO : OD$, and therefore BO bisects the angle ABD. See fig. 1.

vi. If three straight lines, which do not all lie in one plane, be cut in the same ratio by three planes, two of which are parallel, shew that the third will be parallel to the other two, if its intersections with the three straight lines are not all in one straight line.

This may be easily proved by a "reductio ad absurdum."

vii. Define a parabola: and prove from the definition that it cannot be cut by a straight line in more than two points.

For if possible let a straight line cut the parabola in three points P, Q, R, and let it cut the directrix in T. Draw Pp, Qq, Rr perpendiculars to the directrix, and let S be the focus. Then since $SP = Pp$, $SQ = Qq$, it follows that $SP : SQ :: PT : QT$, and therefore ST bisects the exterior angle to PSQ. Similarly ST also bisects the exterior angle to PSR. Which is absurd.

viii. P, Q are points in two confocal ellipses, at which the line joining the common foci subtends equal angles; prove that the tangents at P, Q are inclined at an angle which is equal to the angle subtended by PQ at either focus.

Let the normals at P and Q meet in G, join QP and produce it to any point R. Then the angle between the tangents is equal to the angle PGQ which is

$$= RPG - RQG = (RPS - RQS) + (SPG - SQG).$$

Now $SPG = SQG$, being the halves of equal angles, and the difference $RPS - RQS = PSQ$. Similarly the angle PGQ may be proved $= PHQ$.

ix. If a circle, passing through Y and Z, touch the major axis in Q, and that diameter of the circle, which passes through Q, meet the tangent in P, then $PQ = BC$.

Let the tangent YZ cut the major axis in T. Then by similar triangles

$$\frac{PQ}{QT} = \frac{SY}{YT} \text{ and } \frac{PQ}{QT} = \frac{HZ}{ZT}; \therefore \frac{PQ^2}{QT^2} = \frac{SY.HZ}{TY.TZ}.$$

But $TY.TZ = TQ^2$ by Euclid, III. 36, and $SY.HZ = BC^2$;

$$\therefore PQ = BC.$$

11. In an hyperbola, supposing the two asymptotes and one point of the curve to be given in position, shew how to construct the curve; and find the position of the foci.

Let OX, OY be the two asymptotes, and P the given point. Draw PN parallel to OY cutting OX in N. Measure $OD = OE$ along the asymptotes, such that $OD^2 = 4.ON.NP$. Bisect the angle DOE by OA cutting DE in A. Then OA, AD are equal to the axes; and the remainder of the construction is obvious.

12. Given a right cone and a point within it, there are but two sections which have this point for focus; and the planes of these sections make equal angles with the straight line joining the given point and the vertex of the cone.

Let V be the vertex, VCO the axis of the given cone, and P the given point. Then, if two spheres be inscribed in the cone and passing through P, the tangent planes to these spheres will evidently be the only two sections whose foci are at P. Let C and O be the centres of the two spheres, then $VC : VO :: CL : OM :: CP : PO$; therefore VP bisects the angle exterior to CPO in the triangle CPO. But the radii CP, PO are perpendicular to the sections AB, DE, therefore VP bisects the angle between these sections. See fig. 2.

TUESDAY, *Jan.* 3. 1½ *to* 4.

SENIOR MODERATOR. Arabic numbers.
JUNIOR EXAMINER. Roman numbers.

4. (3) SOLVE the equations,

$$x^2 - yz = a^2, \quad y^2 - zx = b^2, \quad z^2 - xy = c^2.$$

Multiplying the second and third of these equations together, and subtracting the square of the first, we get

$$x(3xyz - x^3 - y^3 - z^3) = b^2c^2 - a^4;$$

therefore by symmetry

$$\frac{x}{a^4 - b^2c^2} = \frac{y}{b^4 - c^2a^2} = \frac{z}{c^4 - a^2b^2} = \lambda, \text{ say.}$$

Hence, substituting in the first equation,

$$\lambda^2(a^6 + b^6 + c^6 - 3a^2b^2c^2) = 1;$$

therefore

$$x = \pm \frac{a^4 - b^2c^2}{(a^6 + b^6 + c^6 - 3a^2b^2c^2)^{\frac{1}{2}}},$$

$$y = \pm \frac{b^4 - c^2a^2}{(a^6 + b^6 + c^6 - 3a^2b^2c^2)^{\frac{1}{2}}},$$

$$z = \pm \frac{c^4 - a^2b^2}{(a^6 + b^6 + c^6 - 3a^2b^2c^2)^{\frac{1}{2}}}.$$

viii. Trace the changes in sign of $\dfrac{\sin(\pi \cos \theta)}{\cos(\pi \sin \theta)}$, as θ varies from 0 to π.

The numerator is positive when θ lies between 0 and $\dfrac{\pi}{2}$, and negative when θ lies between $\dfrac{\pi}{2}$ and π.

The denominator is positive when θ lies between 0 and $\dfrac{\pi}{6}$, negative when θ lies between $\dfrac{\pi}{6}$ and $\dfrac{5\pi}{6}$, and positive when θ lies between $\dfrac{5\pi}{6}$ and π.

Hence the expression is positive from 0 to $\dfrac{\pi}{6}$,

,, negative ,, $\dfrac{\pi}{6}$ to $\dfrac{\pi}{2}$,

,, positive ,, $\dfrac{\pi}{2}$ to $\dfrac{5\pi}{6}$,

,, negative ,, $\dfrac{5\pi}{6}$ to π.

Prove that,
$$\sin 3(A-15) = 4\cos(A-45)\cos(A+15)\sin(A-15),$$
and find $\sin A$ and $\sin B$ from the equations,
$$a \sin^2 A + b \sin^2 B = C,$$
$$a \sin 2A - b \sin 2B = 0,$$
(1) $\qquad \sin 3A = 3 \sin A - 4 \sin^3 A,$
$\qquad \cos 3A = 4 \cos^3 A - 3 \cos A\,;$

$\therefore \sin 3A - \cos 3A$
$\quad = (\sin A + \cos A)\{3 - 4(\sin^2 A + \cos^2 A - \sin A \cos A)\},$
$\quad = 2 \sin 45 \cos(A-45)\{2 \sin 2A - 1\},$
$\quad = 4 \sin 45 \cos(A-45)\{\sin 2A - \sin 30\},$
$\quad = 8 \sin 45 \cos(A-45) \sin(A-15) \cos(A+15).$

But $\quad \sin 3A - \cos 3A = \sin 3A - \sin(90 - 3A)$
$\qquad\qquad = 2 \cos 45 \sin(3A - 45)\,;$

$\therefore \sin 3(A-15) = 4\cos(A-45)\sin(A-15)\cos(A+15).$

(2) $\quad a\sin^2 A + b\sin^2 B = c,$

$\qquad a^2\sin^2 A \cos^2 A = b^2 \sin^2 B \cos^2 B,$

$\qquad a^2\sin^2 A - b^2\sin^2 B = a^2\sin^4 A - b^2\sin^4 B$

$\qquad\qquad = c(a\sin^2 A - b\sin^2 B);$

$\therefore a(a-c)\sin^2 A = b(b-c)\sin^2 B;$

$\therefore ab(b-c) + ab(a-c) = \dfrac{bc(b-c)}{\sin^2 A} = \dfrac{ac(a-c)}{\sin^2 B};$

$\therefore \sin^2 A = \dfrac{bc(b-c)}{ab(a+b-2c)} = \dfrac{c(b-c)}{a(a+b-2c)},$

$\quad \sin^2 B = \dfrac{ac(a-c)}{ab(a+b-2c)} = \dfrac{c(a-c)}{b(a+b-2c)},$

whence, &c.

xii. A railway passenger seated in one corner of the carriage looks out of the windows at the further end and observes that a star near the horizon is traversing these windows in the direction of the train's motion and that it is obscured by the partition between the corner window on his own side of the carriage and the middle window while the train is moving through the seventh part of a mile. Shew that the train is on a curve the concavity of which is directed towards the star, and which, if it be circular, has a radius of nearly three miles; the length of the carriage being seven feet and the breadth of the partition four inches.

Owing to the great distance of the star, the motion of the carriage parallel to itself has no effect upon the point in which the line joining the star and the passenger's eye meets the window. Hence since this line meets the window in points which move in the direction of the carriage's motion, the direction of the carriage must be continually varying, and the carriage must be on a curve concave to the star. The rest of the question is too obvious for explanation.

xiii. If a, b, and B be given, shew under what circum-

WEDNESDAY, *Jan.* 4. 9 *to* 12.

SENIOR MODERATOR. Arabic numbers.
JUNIOR EXAMINER. Roman numbers.

1. ENUNCIATE the proposition of the parallelogram of forces; and, assuming its truth for the *magnitude*, prove it also for the *direction*, of the resultant.

Let AB and AC represent two forces acting on the point A. Complete the parallelogram AD, then by hypothesis AD represents the resultant in magnitude; it is required to prove that AD represents the resultant in direction also. Fig. 4.

Draw AD' in the direction of the resultant and equal to it and therefore also equal to AD. Complete the parallelogram $AD'EC$ and draw the diagonal AE.

AD', AB and AC represent three forces in equilibrium, each of them is therefore equal and opposite to the resultant of the other two. But by hypothesis AE is equal to the resultant of AD' and AC.

Therefore AE is equal to AB and therefore to CD.

Also EC is equal to AD' and therefore to AD.

Hence the quadrilateral $AECD$ has its opposite sides equal, it is therefore a parallelogram; therefore EC is parallel to AD.

But EC is also parallel to AD'; therefore AD' and AD are in the same straight line.

2. Two equal particles, each attracting with a force varying directly as the distance, are situated at the opposite extremities

of a diameter of a horizontal circle, on whose circumference a small smooth ring is capable of sliding; prove that the ring will be kept at rest in any position under the attraction of the particles.

Let A and B be the particles at opposite extremities of the diameter AB, and let P be the attracted ring. Join AP, BP. These lines represent the forces on P, and the resultant force is therefore in the direction of that diagonal of the parallelogram on AP, PB which passes through P. Hence the resultant passes through O the centre of the circle since the diagonals of parallelograms bisect each other, and therefore the reaction of the smooth curve is capable of counteracting the resultant force wherever P may be situated.

3. Two equal heavy particles are situated at the extremities of the latus rectum of a parabolic arc without weight, which is placed with its vertex in contact with that of an equal parabola, whose axis is vertical and concavity downwards; prove that the parabolic arc may be turned through any angle without disturbing its equilibrium, provided no sliding be possible between the curves.

In the figure, fig. 5, it follows from the equality of the parabolas that the arcs AP and $A'P$, and the angles ASP and $A'S'P$ are equal, and that the tangent at P bisects the angle SPS'. But the tangent at P bisects the angle between SP and the line through P parallel to the axis AS. Hence PS' is parallel to AS and therefore vertical.

Hence the perpendiculars from P upon the verticals through L and L' the extremities of the latus rectum are always equal, and therefore equal weights at these points always balance about P.

4. Find the position of equilibrium when a common balance is loaded with given unequal weights.

If the tongue of the balance be very slightly out of adjustment, prove that the true weight of a body is the arithmetic mean of its apparent weights, when weighed in the opposite scales.

Generally $\tan\theta = \dfrac{(P-Q)a}{(P+Q)h + Wh}$.

In this case the beam appears horizontal when it is really inclined at a very small angle α to the horizon. If then P be the true weight, W and W' the apparent weights,

$$P - W = \{(P+W)h + Wk\}\tan\alpha,$$
$$W' - P = \{(P+W')h + Wk\}\tan\alpha,$$

and we may consider W and W' as equal in the coefficients of the very small quantity $\tan\alpha$;

$$\therefore P - W = W' - P \text{ approximately,}$$
$$P = \frac{W+W'}{2}.$$

5. In the figure of Euclid, Book I. Prop. 47, if the perimeters of the squares be regarded as physical lines uniform throughout, prove that the figure will balance about the middle point of the hypothenuse with that line horizontal the lines of construction having no weight.

Let D be the middle point of AB, and DNE, DMF perpendiculars from D bisecting the sides AC and CB in N and M. See fig. 6.

Then
$$DE = EN + ND$$
$$= \tfrac{1}{2}AC + \tfrac{1}{2}CB$$
$$= DF.$$

Therefore the perpendiculars from D upon the verticals through E and F are proportional to the cosines of the angles EDA and FDB respectively, and are therefore proportional to BC and AC respectively, i.e. to the weights of the perimeters of the squares acting at F and E respectively.

Hence these weights balance about D when AB is horizontal, and it is clear that the weight of the perimeter on AB passes through D; therefore the whole balances about this point.

6. A uniform heavy rod, having one extremity attached to a fixed point, about which it is free to move in all directions, passes over the circumference of a rough ring whose

centre is at the fixed point and whose plane is inclined at a given angle to the horizon; find the limiting position of equilibrium.

Let O be the centre of the ring, fig. 7. OH the line of greatest slope through O in the plane of the ring and inclined to the horizon at the angle α, OB the rod, acting on the circle at C.

Let $2a$ be the length of the rod,

b ...... radius of the ring,

θ ...... angle HOB,

μ the coefficient of friction, W the weight of the rod, and R the normal action at C.

We may replace W acting at G by $\dfrac{W(r-a)}{r}$ at O and $W\dfrac{a}{r}$ at C, and this latter by $W\dfrac{a}{r}\cos\alpha$, perpendicular to the plane of ring, and $W\dfrac{a}{r}\sin\alpha$ along this plane;

$$\therefore R = W\frac{a}{r}\cos\alpha \quad \text{and} \quad \mu R = W\frac{a}{r}\sin\alpha\sin\theta,$$

resolving perpendicular to rod; therefore by division

$$\sin\theta = \mu\cot\alpha.$$

vii. A point, moving with a uniform acceleration, describes 20 feet in the half-second which elapses after the first second of its motion; compare its acceleration with that of a falling heavy particle; and give its numerical measure, taking a minute as the unit of time, and a mile as that of space.

Let a be the numerical measure of the acceleration of the point, taking a foot as the unit of space, and half-a-second as that of time.

Then it will describe $\dfrac{a}{2}$ feet in the first half-second.

At the end of this time it will have a velocity, which, if it continued uniform during the next half-second, would carry it over a feet.

At the end of the first second, its velocity will be twice as great as at the end of the first half-second; that is, a velocity which if it continued uniform during the next half-second, would carry the point over $2a$ feet. In consequence of the acceleration, it will move over $\dfrac{a}{2}$ feet more, or $\dfrac{5a}{2}$ feet. Hence

$$\frac{5a}{2} = 20,$$

or $a = 8$.

Hence, taking a second as the unit of time, and a foot as the unit of space, the numerical measure of the acceleration will be 32; that is,

acceleration of this point : acceleration of falling particle

$$:: 32 : 32 \cdot 2$$
$$:: 160 : 161.$$

If a minute be the unit of time, and a mile that of space, the acceleration will be measured by

$$\frac{32 \times 60^2}{5280} = \frac{32 \times 15}{22}$$
$$= \frac{240}{11}.$$

ix. A heavy particle slides down a smooth inclined plane of given height; prove that the time of its descent varies as the secant of the inclination of the plane to the vertical.

Let h be the height of the plane, α its inclination to the vertical, then its length will be $h \sec \alpha$, and the acceleration down the plane $g \cos \alpha$;

∴ if T be the time of descent

$$\frac{g \cos \alpha \cdot T^2}{2} = h \sec \alpha,$$

or $T^2 = 2gh \cdot \sec^2 \alpha$;

∴ $T = (2gh)^{\frac{1}{2}} \sec \alpha$,

or $T \propto \sec \alpha$,

x. A heavy particle is projected from a given point with a given velocity, so as to pass through another given point; prove that, in general, there will be two parabolic paths which the particle may describe; and give a geometrical construction to determine their foci. Also find the locus of the second point in order that there may be only one parabolic path.

Since the velocity of projection is given, the directrix of the parabolic path is given.

Let MN be the directrix, P the point of projection, Q the point through which the particle is to pass. Fig. 8.

Draw PM, QN, perpendicular to MN. With P, Q as centres and PM, QN as radii, describe two circles; these will in general intersect in two points S, S', which will be the foci of the two parabolic paths.

If, however, the two circles touch one another, there will be but one parabolic path. In order that this may be the case, we must have

$$QN + PM = PQ.$$

Hence if QN be produced to K, so that NK may be equal to PM, and KK' be drawn parallel to MN, we shall have

$$\text{distance of } Q \text{ from } KK' = PQ,$$

or, the locus of Q is a parabola, of which P is the focus, and KK' the directrix.

xi. A series of perfectly elastic balls are arranged in the same straight line, one of them impinges directly on the next, and so on; prove that, if their masses form a geometrical progression of which the common ratio is 2, their velocities after impact will form a geometrical progression of which the common ratio is $\frac{4}{9}$.

Let M, $2M$, be the masses of two adjacent balls, v the velocity of M before impact, u_1, u_2, the respective velocities of M, $2M$, after impact, then we have to prove that $u_2 = \frac{2}{3} v$.

Now the momentum is the same before and after impact;

$$\therefore Mu_1 + 2Mu_2 = Mv \quad \text{(1)},$$

and since the balls are perfectly elastic, the *vis viva* is unaltered;

$$\therefore Mu_1^2 + 2Mu_2^2 = Mv^2 \quad\ldots\ldots\ldots\ldots\ldots (2).$$

Squaring (1) and multiplying (2) by M, we get

$$(u_1 + 2u_2)^2 = u_1^2 + 2u_2^2;$$

$$\therefore 2u_1 + u_2 = 0.$$

Hence eliminating u_1 by (1),

$$\frac{3u_2}{2} = v;$$

$$\therefore u_2 = \frac{2v}{3}.$$

WEDNESDAY, *Jan.* 4. 1½ *to* 4.

JUNIOR MODERATOR. Arabic numbers.
SENIOR EXAMINER. Roman numbers.

1. A UNIFORM tube is bent into the form of a parabola, and placed with its vertex downwards and axis vertical: supposing any quantities of two fluids of densities ρ, ρ' to be poured into it, and r, r' to be the distances of the two free surfaces respectively from the focus, then the distance of the common surface from the focus will be $\dfrac{r\rho - r'\rho'}{\rho - \rho'}$.

This follows at once from the two principles:

(1) If two fluids be placed in a bent tube, the altitudes of the free surfaces above the common surface are inversely as their densities.

(2) The distance of any point of a parabola from the focus is equal to its distance from the directrix.

2. A parallelogram is immersed in a fluid with one side in the surface; shew how to draw a line from one extremity of this side dividing the parallelogram into two parts on which the pressures are equal.

Let $ABCD$ be the parallelogram, AE the line drawn from one angle to the base. Then the pressure on the triangle is $= \dfrac{1}{2}$ the pressure on the whole parallelogram. Fig. 9.

Now the pressure $\propto$ area . depth of centre of gravity; the areas of the two figures are as $\dfrac{CE}{2}$: CD; the depths of the centres of gravity are as $\dfrac{2}{3} : \dfrac{1}{2}$;

$$\therefore \dfrac{2}{3} \cdot \dfrac{CE}{2} = \dfrac{1}{2} \cdot \dfrac{1}{2} \, CD;$$

$$\therefore CE = \dfrac{3}{4} \, CD.$$

3. A heavy hollow right cone, closed by a base without weight, is immersed in a fluid, find the force that will sustain it with its axis horizontal.

Let $AB = h$ be the axis of the cone, A the vertex. The forces acting on the cone are, its weight W acting downwards at G the centre of gravity of the surface, $AG = \dfrac{2}{3}h$; and W' the weight of the water displaced acting upwards at H the centre of gravity of the volume, $AH = \dfrac{3}{4}h$.

The resultant of these is $W - W'$ acting at a point C, where

$$(W - W') \, AC = W \cdot \dfrac{2}{3}h - W' \cdot \dfrac{3}{4}h.$$

4. A given weight of heavy elastic fluid of uniform temperature is confined in a smooth vertical cylinder by a piston of given weight; shew how to find the volume of the fluid.

It is proved in Goodwin's *Course*, if pp' be the pressures of the atmosphere at two points whose vertical distance is x, that

$$x = \dfrac{\tau}{\log \left(1 - \dfrac{g\tau}{k}\right)} \cdot \log \dfrac{p}{p'},$$

where τ is the thickness of the very small layers into which the atmosphere was supposed divided.

If W = weight of the piston, A its area, and W' = weight of air contained in the cylinder, then $pA = W$, $p'A = W + W'$, and Ax becomes the volume of the fluid. Hence we have

$$x = \frac{\tau}{\log\left(1 - \frac{g\tau}{k}\right)} \cdot \log \frac{W}{W + W'}.$$

In this equation τ is any very small quantity. If $\tau = 0$ it is proved in the *Course* cited above, that the expression for x becomes

$$x = \frac{k}{g} \cdot \log \frac{W + W'}{W}.$$

5. If A be the area of the section of each pump of the fire engine, l the length of the down stroke, n the number of strokes per minute, B the area of the hose, then it is obvious that the average velocity from the hose, when both pumps work, $= \dfrac{2Aln}{B}$.

6. Supposing some light material, whose density is ρ, to be weighed by means of weights of density ρ', the density of the atmosphere when the barometer stands at 30 inches being unity; shew that, if the mercury in the barometer fall one inch, the material will appear to be altered by

$$\frac{\rho' - \rho}{(\rho - 1)(30\rho' - 29)}$$

of its former weight. Will it appear to weigh more or less?

Let v = volume of the material, V the volume of the weight; then V measures the apparent weight of the material, and we have

$$V(\rho' - 1) = v(\rho - 1).$$

When the barometer has fallen one inch, the density of the air has become $\dfrac{29}{30}$, and in this state let V' be the volume of the weight required to balance the same material. Then

$$V'\left(\rho' - \frac{29}{30}\right) = v\left(\rho - \frac{29}{30}\right);$$

$$\therefore \frac{V'-V}{V} = \frac{\rho'-\rho}{(30\rho'-29)(\rho-1)}.$$

IX. A bright point is at the bottom of still water, and an eye is vertically above it, at the same distance from the surface; if a small isosceles prism, of which the refractive angle i is nearly two right angles, be interposed so as to have its base in contact with the water, prove that the angular distance between the images of the point in the two faces is

$$\frac{\mu-1}{\mu'-1}(\pi-i),$$

μ', μ being the refractive indices for water and for the prism respectively.

Let a ray diverge from the bright point Q, and after passing through the prism enter the centre of the eye E. Then this ray makes equal angles (ϕ) with the vertical before and after refraction, because the eye and Q are at equal distances from the surface of the water. Imagine a very thin layer of air to be placed between the prism and the surface, the deviation of a ray on entering this layer will be $-(\mu'-1)\phi$. The deviation on passing through the prism will be

$$(\mu-1)\frac{\pi-i}{2}.$$

Hence the total deviation will be

$$(\mu-1)\frac{\pi-i}{2} - (\mu'-1)\phi.$$

But the total deviation of a ray is the sum of the acute angles it makes with the vertical before and after refraction, which is 2ϕ. Hence equating these, we get

$$2\phi = \frac{\mu-1}{\mu'+1}(\pi-i).$$

X. Prove that, as the focus of an incident convergent pencil moves from a concave lens, the distance between the conjugate foci always increases, except when the focus of incident rays passes between the distances f and $2f$ from the lens.

In a convergent pencil converging to a distance u,

$$\frac{1}{v} = \frac{1}{f} - \frac{1}{u}.$$

As $\qquad$ u increases from 0 to f,

$\qquad\qquad v$ .... $0 ... \infty$,

$\qquad (-v) - u$ .... $0 ... \infty$.

As $\qquad$ u increases from f to $2f$,

$\qquad\qquad v$ is positive and decreases from ∞ to $2f$,

and $\qquad\qquad v + u$ .... $\infty ... 4f$.

As $\qquad$ u increases from $2f$ to ∞,

$\qquad\qquad v$ decreases ...... $2f ... 0$,

$\qquad\qquad v + u$ increases ...... $4f ... \infty$.

xi. If the focal length of a convex lens be 3 inches, and the shortest distance of distinct vision be 6 inches, prove that, when the eye is always placed so as to see distinctly under the greatest possible angle, the lens magnifies when within 6 inches of the object, and diminishes at greater distances.

If PQ be the object on the axis, CQ of the lens.   Fig. 10.

$\dfrac{PQ}{6}$ = greatest angle with the naked eye.

I. When the image is on the same side as PQ, let pq be the image;

$$\therefore \frac{1}{Cq} = \frac{1}{CQ} - \frac{1}{3}.$$

(1) Let $\quad Cq < 6$; $\therefore \dfrac{1}{CQ} > \dfrac{1}{3} + \dfrac{1}{6}$ or $\dfrac{1}{2}$;

$\therefore$ ratio of apparent angles $= \dfrac{pq}{PQ} = \dfrac{Cq}{CQ} > 1.$

(2) Let $\qquad Cq > 6$, or $CQ > 2$,

then the greatest angle, with lens, $= \dfrac{pq}{Cq}$,

ratio of apparent angles $= \dfrac{pq}{PQ} \cdot \dfrac{6}{Cq} = \dfrac{6}{CQ} > 1$.

II. When the image is on the opposite side, as $p'q'$,

ratio of apparent angles $= \dfrac{p'q'}{PQ} = \dfrac{Cq'}{CQ}$,

and $\dfrac{1}{Cq'} = \dfrac{1}{3} - \dfrac{1}{CQ}$, $CQ > 3$;

∴ the ratio $= \dfrac{3}{CQ-3} > 1$ if $CQ < 6$,

< 1 if $CQ > 6$.

xii. If the object-glass be divided, so as to form two semi-circular lenses, and these be displaced along the line of division, what must be the displacement of the centres in order that a double star may appear as three stars?

This is the combination devised to cause a duplication of an image, and called the Heliometer.

Each half forms an image of each star, S, S', and S, S'', and if one of each pair coincide at S, the double star appears as three stars. See Figs. 11 and 12.

If α be the number of seconds in the angular distance of the stars, F the focal length of each semi-lens, the distance of the centres C, C' will subtend at the middle of the three images of the stars an angle $CSC' = \alpha''$;

∴ the distance of the centres $= F\alpha \sin 1''$.

THURSDAY, *Jan.* 5. 9 *to* 12.

SENIOR MODERATOR. Roman numbers.
JUNIOR MODERATOR. Arabic numbers.

i. THREE concentric circles are drawn in the same plane. Draw a straight line, such that one of its segments between the inner and outer circumference may be bisected at one of the points in which the line meets the middle circumference.

Let O be the common centre. Take any point P on the circumference of the middle circle; join OP and produce to Q making $PQ = OP$. With centre Q and radius equal to that of the smallest circle describe a circle, and let one of the points in which it meets the outermost circle be R. Again, with centre Q and radius equal to that of the largest circle describe a circle, and let one of the points in which it meets the innermost circle be S. Then if R and S be taken properly RP and PS shall be in one straight line which line will also satisfy the required condition. Fig. 13.

Join OR, QS, OS, QR.

Then $ORQS$ is a parallelogram, because its opposite sides are equal, and from this, together with the property that diagonals of a parallelogram bisect each other, the truth of the proposition is obvious.

ii. If a quadrilateral circumscribes an ellipse, prove that either pair of opposite sides subtends supplementary angles at either focus.

Let $ABCD$ be the quadrilateral; P, Q, R, T the points of contact of the respective sides, and S one of one foci. Fig. 14.

Join S with the angles of the quadrilateral and the points of contact.

By a property of the ellipse $ASP = TSA$, applying this to the eight angles at S taken in pairs, we get

$$ASB + DSC = ASD + BSC;$$

and since all the angles at S are together equal to four right angles the truth of the proposition is evident.

iii. If a polygon of a given number of sides circumscribes an ellipse, prove that, when its area is a minimum, any side is parallel to the line joining the points of contact of the two adjacent sides.

The polygon of minimum area and given number of sides circumscribing a circle is the regular polygon, and any side is therefore parallel to the line joining the points of contact of the two adjacent sides.

Hence by projecting this circle into an ellipse the truth of the proposition is obvious.

Or we may prove it thus: Fig. 15.

Let EA, AB, BF be three consecutive sides of the polygon. Then if the area is a minimum a small displacement given to AB while EA and DF remain fixed cannot alter the area of the polygon. Let AB be displaced to $A'B'$. The point of intersection of these lines will ultimately coincide with the point of contact P, and we have

$$\triangle APA' = \triangle BPB' \text{ ultimately};$$
$$\therefore AP \cdot A'P \sin APA' = BP \cdot B'P \sin BPB',$$
$$AP \cdot A'P = BP \cdot B'P;$$
$$\therefore AP = BP,$$

since $A'P$ and $B'P$ are ultimately equal to AP and BP respectively.

Hence the diameter which bisects chords parallel to EF meets the ellipse in P, and therefore the tangent at P is parallel to EF.

4. If the tangent at any point P of an hyperbola cut an asymptote in T, and if SP cut the same asymptote in Q, then $SQ = QT$. See Fig. 16.

If from any point T, two tangents are drawn to a conic, they subtend equal angles at either focus. One of these tangents in this problem becomes an asymptote, the other is TP. Therefore if SR be drawn parallel to QT, the angles TSQ, TSR are equal, and therefore the angles QST, QTS are equal, or $SQ = QT$.

5. Prove that the sum of the products of the first n natural numbers taken two and two together is

$$\frac{(n-1)n(n+1)(3n+2)}{24}.$$

Since

$$(a+b+c+\ldots)^2 = a^2+b^2+c^2+\ldots+2(ab+bc+\ldots),$$

let $a = 1$, $b = 2$, $c = 3$, &c. ..., then we have the sum of the products

$$= \frac{1}{2}\left\{\left(n \cdot \frac{n-1}{2}\right)^2 - \frac{n \cdot (n+1)(2n+1)}{6}\right\},$$

which reduces to $\dfrac{(n-1)n \cdot (n+1)(3n+2)}{24}$.

6. The centres of the escribed circles of a triangle must lie without the circumscribing circle, and cannot be equidistant from it unless the triangle be equilateral.

It may be proved, as in Todhunter's *Trigonometry* (Art. 253), if Q be the centre of the circumscribing circle, P of any one of the escribed circles, and R, r_1 their radii, that $PQ^2 = R^2 + 2Rr_1$; whence it follows that PQ must be greater than R, and the three distances cannot be equal, unless the radii of the escribed circles are equal. The formulæ for these radii are respectively $\dfrac{\Delta}{S-a}$, $\dfrac{\Delta}{S-b}$, $\dfrac{\Delta}{S-c}$, where a, b, c are the sides and Δ the area of the triangle. Whence it follows that a, b, c are all equal.

This may also be proved independently of the proposition quoted from Todhunter.

vii. If perpendiculars be drawn from the angles of an equilateral triangle upon any tangent to the inscribed circle, prove that the sum of the reciprocals of those perpendiculars which fall upon the same side of the tangent is equal to the reciprocal of that perpendicular which falls upon the opposite side.

Let ABC be the triangle, O the centre of the inscribed circle, and P be the point of contact of the tangent in question so that OP makes the angle θ with AO, (O being the centre of the circle). Fig. 17.

Then the inclinations of OB and OC to OP produced are

$$\frac{\pi}{3} - \theta, \text{ and } \frac{\pi}{3} + \theta.$$

Hence remembering that in this case the radius of the circumscribing circle $= 2$ the radius of the inscribed $= 2r$, suppose perpendicular from $A = 2r \cos\theta - r = r(2\cos\theta - 1)$,

$$\ldots\ldots\ldots\ldots\ldots B = 2r\cos\left(\frac{\pi}{3} - \theta\right) + r = r\left\{2\cos\left(\frac{\pi}{3} - \theta\right) + 1\right\}$$

$$\ldots\ldots\ldots\ldots\ldots C = 2r\cos\left(\frac{\pi}{3} + \theta\right) + r = r\left\{2\cos\left(\frac{\pi}{3} + \theta\right) + 1\right\}$$

and

$$\frac{1}{2\cos\left(\frac{\pi}{3} + \theta\right) + 1} + \frac{1}{2\cos\left(\frac{\pi}{3} - \theta\right) + 1} = \frac{1}{2\cos\theta - 1},$$

for

$$\frac{1}{(2\cos\theta + 1) - \sqrt{3}\sin\theta} + \frac{1}{(\cos\theta + 1) + \sqrt{3}\sin\theta}$$

$$= \frac{2(\cos\theta + 1)}{1 + \cos^2\theta - 3\sin^2\theta + 2\cos\theta}$$

$$= \frac{2(\cos\theta + 1)}{4\cos^2\theta + 2\cos\theta - 2} = \frac{\cos\theta + 1}{2\cos^2\theta + \cos\theta - 1}$$

$$= \frac{\cos\theta + 1}{(2\cos\theta - 1)(\cos\theta + 1)} = \frac{1}{2\cos\theta - 1}.$$

viii. Four equal particles are mutually repulsive, the law of force being that of the inverse distance. If they be joined together by four strings of given length so as to form a quadrilateral, prove that, when there is equilibrium, the four particles lie in a circle. Fig. 18.

When there is equilibrium, the action of C on A : action of B on A

:: $\sin DAB$: $\sin DAC$,

also action of D on B : action of A on B

:: $\sin ABC$: $\sin DBC$;

∴ action of C on A : action of D on B

:: $\sin DAB . \sin DBC$: $\sin DAC . \sin ABC$;

∴ DB : AC :: $\sin DAB \sin DBC$: $\sin DAC \sin ABC$.

(It is to be observed that the action between A and B is the difference between the repulsive force and the tension, it therefore follows no law);

∴ $\dfrac{AB \sin DAB}{\sin ADB}$: $\dfrac{AB \sin ABC}{\sin ACB}$

:: $\sin DAB . \sin DBC$: $\sin DAC \sin ABC$,

$\sin ACB$: $\sin ADB$ :: $\sin DBC$: $\sin DAC$;

∴ $\dfrac{BO . \sin DBC}{OC}$: $\dfrac{AO \sin DAC}{OD}$ :: $\sin DBC$: $\sin DAC$;

∴ $BO . OD = AO . OC$, whence, &c.

9. A heavy rod is placed in any manner resting on two points A and B of a rough horizontal curve, and a string attached to the middle point C of the chord is pulled in any direction so that the rod is on the point of motion. Prove that the locus of the intersection of the string with the directions of the frictions at the points of support is an arc of a circle and a part of a straight line.

Find also how the force must be applied that its intersections with the frictions may trace out the remainder of the circle. See Fig. 19.

First, let the rod be on point of slipping at both A and B, and let F, F'' be the frictions at the two points. Then F, F'' are both known, and depend only on the weight and the position of the centre of gravity of the rod. Since there is equilibrium the two frictions and the tension must meet in one point, let this be P. Then since $AC = CB$, it is evident that CP is half the diagonal of the parallelogram whose sides are AP, PB; hence by the triangle of forces, AP, PB, and $2 \cdot PC$ will respectively represent the forces in those directions. Hence $AP : PB :: F : F''$ and are therefore in a constant ratio. Therefore the locus of P is a circle.

The string CP cuts the circle in *two* points, but the forces can meet in only one of these. It is evident that the rod must be on the point of turning about some one point as a centre, which point O is the intersection of the perpendiculars drawn to PA, PB at A and B. Now the frictions, in order to balance the tension must act *towards* P and therefore the directions of motion of A and B must be *from* P. This clearly cannot be the case unless the point O is on the same side of the line AB as P. Therefore the angle PAB is greater than a right angle. Thus the point P cannot lie on the dotted part of the circle.

Secondly. Let the rod be on the point of slipping at one point of support only. Then since the centre of gravity is nearer B than A, the rod will slip at A, and turn round B as a fixed point. Thus the friction acts along QA, and the locus of P is the fixed straight line QA.

But P cannot lie on the dotted part of the straight line, for if possible let it be at R. Then if AR represents F, RB must be less than F'' because there is no slipping at B. But because R lies within the circle, the ratio $\dfrac{AR}{RB}$ is $< \dfrac{AP}{PB}$, i.e. $< \dfrac{F}{F''}$ and therefore $RB > F''$ and therefore the rod has moved at B which is contrary to supposition. Thus the string being produced will always cut the arc of the circle and the part of the straight line in one point and one point only, and the frictions always tend towards that point when the rod is on the point of motion.

In order that the locus of P may be the dotted part of the circle, it is necessary that the frictions should tend one from

P and the other to P, and the tension must therefore act in the angle between PA and PB produced. By the triangle of forces APB we see that the tension must act parallel to AB and be proportional to it.

x. A rigid wire without appreciable mass is formed into an arc of an equiangular spiral and carries a small heavy particle fixed in its pole. If the convexity of the wire be placed in contact with a perfectly rough horizontal plane, prove that the point of contact with the plane will move with uniform acceleration, and find this acceleration.

Let P be the point of contact at any instant and S the corresponding position of the pole.

Since the curve rolls on the line the instantaneous direction of the motion of S is perpendicular to SP, i.e. SP is the normal to the path described by S at S.

But SP is always parallel to itself by the property of the spiral, and therefore the path of S is a straight line inclined at the angle $\frac{\pi}{2} - \alpha$ to the horizon, where α is the constant angle between the tangent and radius vector.

Hence the heavy particle is constrained to move along this line, and the acceleration of gravity resolved in the direction of the particle's motion is $g \cos \alpha$.

If S' and P' be consecutive positions of S and P respectively, it is clear that $PP' : SS' :: 1 : \sin \alpha$;

∴ acceleration of P is $\dfrac{g \cos \alpha}{\sin \alpha} = g \cot \alpha$.

11. If two parabolas be placed with their axes vertical, vertices downwards, and foci coincident, prove that there are three chords down which the time of descent of a particle under the action of gravity from one curve to the other is a minimum, and that one of these is the principal diameter and the other two make an angle of 60° with it on either side. See Figs. 20 and 21.

The chord PQ down which a particle will slide in the least time from a given point P to a given curve CD, makes equal angles with the vertical and the normal to the given curve at the point Q where the chord cuts the curve. For the chord PQ will clearly be found by describing a circle to touch the curve in Q and the centre O of which shall be vertically under P. Then it is evident that PQ makes equal angles with the normal QO and with the vertical PO.

Similarly it may be proved, that the chord of shortest descent PQ from any curve AB to a fixed point Q, makes equal angles with the normal at P and with the vertical.

Again, if PQ be the chord of quickest descent from any curve AB to any other curve CD, by considering P fixed and Q variable, it is evident that PQ makes equal angles with the normal at Q and with the vertical. Also by considering P variable and Q fixed, it is evident that PQ makes equal angles with the normal at P and with the vertical. Hence the normals at P and Q must be parallel.

Now the parabolas in the problem are similar, and have their foci coincident, therefore the normals to the two parabolas at the extremities of any radius vector through the focus are parallel, and no others are parallel. Hence the chord of quickest descent passes through the focus.

First. To find the chord of quickest descent from the outer to the inner. We must have the angle $SQG =$ the angle GSQ, and therefore $GQ = GS$. But $SG = SQ$; therefore the triangle GSQ is equilateral, and the angle $GSQ = 60°$. Fig. 22.

Secondly. To find the chord of quickest descent from the inner to the outer. We must have the angle $GQS =$ the exterior angle QSA, which is impossible unless SQ coincides with the axis.

12. If a particle slide along a chord of a circle under the action of a centre of force varying as the distance, the time will be the same for all chords provided they terminate at either extremity of the diameter through the centre of force. See Figs. 23 and 24.

If a particle describe an ellipse about a centre of force in the centre C, the time of describing any arc AP from the vertex A is known to be measured by the angle ACQ, where

QPN is a common ordinate of the ellipse and the auxiliary circle. This proposition is still true when the ellipse degenerates into its major axis and the particle describes the straight line AC. Thus the time of describing AN is measured by $\cos^{-1}\dfrac{CN}{CA}$.

Let AB be any chord, S the centre of force, then, drawing SC perpendicular to AB, the resolved part of the attraction of S on any point P is proportional to CP, and therefore the time of describing AB is measured by $\cos^{-1}\dfrac{CB}{CA}$. But by similar triangles the ratio $\dfrac{CB}{CA}=\dfrac{SB}{SD}$ which is constant. Therefore the time down all chords through B is the same.

13. A hollow cone floats with its vertex downwards in a cylindrical vessel containing water. Determine the equal quantities of water that may be poured into the cone and into the cylinder that the position of the cone in space may be unaltered.

Let AB, CD be the old and new planes of floatation, cutting the cone in EF, HC. The condition that the position of the cone may be unaltered is the volume $HF=\frac{1}{2}$ vol. CB. Fig. 25.

Let $h = OL$ the part originally immersed, $x = LM$ a = radius of cylinder, 2α = angle of cone. Then

$$\pi \tan^2 \alpha \cdot \frac{(h+x)^3 - h^3}{3} = \tfrac{1}{2}\pi a^2 x ;$$

$$\therefore x = -\tfrac{3}{2}h \pm \sqrt{(\tfrac{3}{2}a^2 \cot^2 \alpha - \tfrac{9}{4}h^2)}.$$

The lower sign makes x negative and is inadmissible; this determines the required quantity of water.

xiv. A hemispherical bowl is filled to the brim with fluid, and a rod specifically heavier than the fluid, rests with one end in contact with the concave surface of the bowl, and passes over the rim of the bowl, find an equation for determining the position of equilibrium.

In this case let $2a$ be the length of the rod AC, $2b$ the radius of the bowl whose centre is O, θ the inclination of the rod to the horizon, ρ the relative specific gravity of the rod and the fluid, A and B the points where the rod rests against the concave surface and the rim of the bowl respectively.

The forces acting on the rod are,

(1) A force proportional to $AB(\rho-1)$ vertically downwards through G the middle point of AB.

(2) A force proportional to $BC.\rho$ vertically downwards through H the middle point of BC.

(3) A force R along AO.

(4) A force R' perpendicular to AB at B.

These two last forces obviously intersect in D the other extremity of the diameter through A. Let the vertical through D meet the rod in E. Then for equilibrium taking moments about E,

$$(\rho-1)AB : GE = \rho . BC . EH.$$
$$AB = 2b\cos\theta, \quad BC = 2(a - b\cos\theta),$$
$$EB = \frac{BD^2}{AB} = \frac{b\sin^2\theta}{\cos\theta}.$$

Substituting, we get

$$\cos^3\theta - \tfrac{3}{2}\rho\frac{a}{b}\cos^2\theta + \tfrac{1}{2}(\rho\frac{a^2}{b^2} + 1)\cos\theta + \frac{\rho a}{2b} = 0,$$

a cubic equation, with its last term positive, whence the positions of equilibrium may be found, and from which it appears that the equilibrium can only be possible when all the roots of the equations are real.

xv. A ray of light passes through a medium of which the refractive index at any point is inversely proportional to the distance of that point from a certain plane. Prove that the path of the ray is a circular arc of which the centre is in the above-mentioned plane.

The medium is obviously arranged in planes of equal refracting power and parallel to the plane mentioned in the question.

And it is clear that the path of a ray is in one plane perpendicular to the above-mentioned plane.

Let the plane in which the ray's path lies be the plane of the paper, and let a small portion of the path be RPQ, AB being the intersection of the plane of reference by the plane of the paper and RP, and PQ elementary portions of the path before and after passing through the plane at P, parallel to AB, and which may therefore be considered as small straight lines. PM and QN perpendiculars on AB, QN being produced to L, draw PO perpendicular to PR to meet the line AB in O, and join QO; See Fig. 26.

$$\therefore \frac{\sin POM}{\sin PQL} = \frac{\frac{1}{QN}}{\frac{1}{PM}} = \frac{PM}{QN};$$

$$\therefore \frac{QN}{\sin PQL} = \frac{PM}{\sin POM} = PO.$$

But if the perpendicular to PQ met AB in O' then

$$\frac{QN}{\sin PQL} = QO';$$

$$\therefore QO' = PO,$$

which is impossible unless O and O' coincide.

Therefore the normal to the ray at every point of its path meets the line AB in the same point. Whence, &c.

16. A small bead is projected with any velocity along a circular wire under the action of a force varying inversely as the fifth power of the distance from a centre of force situated in the circumference. Prove that the pressure on the wire is constant.

This is a particular case of a more general proposition. Let a wire be of such a form that a particle, if projected with velocity V', would freely describe it without causing any pressure on the wire; then if the particle be projected with velocity V, the pressure at any point where the radius of curvature is ρ will be $m\dfrac{V^2 - V'^2}{\rho}$. The pressure will therefore vary as the curvature.

For divide the arc into small elements $s_1\, s_2 \ldots s_n$, and let $v_1\, v_2 \ldots v_n$ be the velocities acquired at the end of those arcs; let $F_1\, F_2 \ldots F_n$ be the resolved parts of the impressed forces along the respective tangents. Then when the arcs are very small, we have

$$\left.\begin{array}{l} v_1^2 - V^2 = 2F_1 s_1 \\ v_2^2 - v_1^2 = 2F_2 s_2 \\ v_3^2 - v_2^2 = 2F_3 s_3 \\ \&c. = \&c. \end{array}\right\}; \quad \therefore v_n^2 - V^2 = 2F_1 s_1 + 2F_2 s_2 + \ldots + 2F_n s_n.$$

Let $v_1'\, v_2' \ldots v_n'$ be the corresponding velocities of the particle when freely describing the wire, then by similar reasoning

$$v_n'^2 - V'^2 = 2F_1 s_1 + \ldots + 2F_n s_n\,;$$

$$\therefore v_n^2 - v_n'^2 = V^2 - V'^2.$$

Now the pressure on the wire = Statical Pressure + the centrifugal force $= P + m\dfrac{v_n^2}{\rho}$. But when the particle describes the curve freely, the pressure = 0, therefore $P = -m\dfrac{v_n'^2}{\rho}$.

$$\therefore \text{Pressure} = m\,\dfrac{v_n^2 - v_n'^2}{\rho}$$

$$= m\,\dfrac{V^2 - V'^2}{\rho}.$$

In the case of a circle described under the action of a central force varying as the inverse fifth power, we know by Newton, that the particle if properly projected would not exert any pressure on the wire. Therefore, when otherwise projected, the pressure varies inversely as the radius of curvature, that is, it is constant.

17. A bright spot of white light is viewed through a right cone of glass, the vertex of which is pointed directly

towards the spot. Describe the appearances seen; and prove that, if a section of the locus of the images corresponding to different values of the refractive index be made by a plane through the axis of the cone, it will be a rectangular hyperbola.

Let AB be the axis of the cone, fig. 27, A the vertex, 2α the angle of the cone, h the height, Q the bright spot, $AQ = u$.

By the ordinary optical formulæ it can be easily proved that the image of Q, formed by light of refractive index μ, will be a ring whose radius and position is given by the formulæ

$$\left. \begin{array}{l} qn = (\mu - 1) u \sin \alpha \cos \alpha \\ Bn = \dfrac{u + h + (\mu - 1) u \sin^2 \alpha}{\mu} \end{array} \right\}.$$

Hence

$(qn + u \sin \alpha \cos \alpha)(Bn - u \sin^2 \alpha) = (u \cos^2 \alpha + h) u \sin \alpha \cos \alpha.$

Therefore, by Goodwin's *Conics*, Prop. IX., q lies on a rectangular hyperbola whose asymptotes are parallel and perpendicular to BA. And since the position and magnitude of this hyperbola is independent of μ, all the coloured rings will lie on the surface formed by the revolution of this hyperbola.

xviii. An elastic string passes through a smooth straight tube whose length is the natural length of the string. It is then pulled out equally at both ends until its length is increased by $\sqrt{2}$ times its original length. Two equal perfectly elastic balls are attached to the extremities and projected with equal velocities at right angles to the string, and so as to impinge upon each other. Prove that the time of impact is independent of the velocity of projection, and that after impact each ball will move in a straight line, assuming that the tension of the string is proportional to the extension throughout the motion.

Let AB be the tube, C and D the positions to which the ends of the string are extended.

Each particle describes an ellipse round the corresponding extremity of the tube as centre, the absolute force depending on the material of which the string is composed.

The line CD will coincide with the major or minor axes of the ellipses according to the magnitude of the initially impressed velocity, and the particles will impinge at a point P in the line PE bisecting AB at right angles. See fig. 28.

(1) If CD be the direction of the major axes the arc of the auxiliary circle described by either particle is

$$\pi - \tan^{-1}\frac{a}{b} \cdot \frac{EP}{AE},$$

or $\quad \pi - \tan^{-1}\frac{a}{b} \cdot \frac{b}{a} \cdot \frac{\sqrt{(2.AE^2 - AE^2)}}{AE} = \pi - \tan^{-1} 1 = \frac{3\pi}{4}.$

(2) If CD be the direction of the minor axes, then the corresponding arc of the auxiliary circle is

$$\frac{\pi}{2} + \tan^{-1}\frac{a}{b} \cdot \frac{AE}{EP},$$

or $\quad \dfrac{\pi}{2} + \tan^{-1}\dfrac{a}{b} \cdot \dfrac{AE}{\dfrac{a}{b} \cdot \sqrt{(b^2 - AE^2)}},$

or $\quad \dfrac{\pi}{2} + \tan^{-1} 1 ; \quad (\because b = \sqrt{2} . AE),$

or $\quad \dfrac{3\pi}{4};$

therefore in both cases the time of impact is independent of the velocity of projection. Let the tangents to the two curves before impact at P be PT and PT' meeting AB in T and T';

then $\qquad AT . AE = 2AE^2;$

$\qquad \therefore AT = 2AE,$

$\qquad\qquad = AB;$

therefore T and T' coincide with B and A respectively, and therefore since the velocities parallel to AB are reversed at impact, those perpendicular to AB remaining unaltered, it is clear that the direction of each particle's motion after impact passes through A and B respectively.

xix. A particle is projected along a chord of an ellipse from any point in the curve, and when it again meets the ellipse has a certain impulse towards the centre of the ellipse impressed upon it, causing it again to describe a chord, and so on for any number of times. Prove that, if after a given number of such impulses the particle pass through another given point on the circumference of the curve, the polygonal area so described about the centre is a maximum, when the successive chords are described in equal times.

Since the particle leaves one given point on the curve, and passes through another given point after touching a given number of points on the curve, (see fig. 29); then in order that the polygonal area described about the centre should be a maximum every such triangle as PQR must also be a maximum, P and R being fixed and Q variable. Hence, if we take a point Q' near to Q, the triangle $RQ'P$ must be equal to RQP, and therefore the tangent to the ellipse at Q must be parallel to PR. Hence by the property of the ellipse if QT be the direction of central impulse at Q, QT bisects RP.

Produce PQ to S, making QS equal to PQ. Then RS is parallel to QT.

Now QS represents the original velocity at Q in direction and magnitude, RS represents the direction of the impressed velocity, and QR of the resultant velocity after the central impulse; therefore QR is proportional to the magnitude of the resultant velocity, and therefore time through QR equals time through PQ, and so on.

THURSDAY, *Jan.* 5. 1 *to* 4.

SENIOR EXAMINER. Roman numbers.
JUNIOR EXAMINER. Arabic numbers.

2. ENUNCIATE and prove Newton's tenth Lemma.

If the curve employed in the proof of this Lemma be an arc of a parabola, the axis of which is perpendicular to the straight line on which time is measured, prove that the accelerating effect of the force will vary as the distance from the axis of the parabola.

Let time be measured along the line AN from the point N, and let V be the vertex of the parabola. Then, at the instant corresponding to P, the time is represented by AN, and the velocity by PN. See fig. 30.

Now, if L be the latus rectum of the parabola,

$$PM^2 = L \cdot VM,$$
$$AK^2 = L \cdot VK;$$
$$\therefore PM^2 - AK^2 = L \cdot PN,$$

or $$AN(AK + AN) = L \cdot PN;$$

∴ when P approaches indefinitely near to A

$$\text{limit} \frac{PN}{AN} = \frac{2AK}{L},$$

or varies as the distance of A from the axis of the parabola.

Again, if P be not indefinitely near to A, and P' a point contiguous to P, it may be shewn that the force at P

$$= \operatorname{limit} \frac{P'N' - PN}{NN'}$$

$$= \tan PXN, \text{ if } PX \text{ be the tangent at } P,$$

$$= \frac{2 \cdot VK}{MP}$$

$$= \frac{2 \cdot MP}{L},$$

or varies as the distance of P from the axis.

3. One circle rolls uniformly within another of twice its radius; prove that the resultant acceleration of a particle situated on the circumference of the rolling circle tends to the centre of the fixed circle, and varies as the distance from that centre.

Let O be the centre of the fixed, C of the moving circle, P the point, the acceleration of which is required. See fig. 31.

Now P describes a circle uniformly round C while C describes a circle of equal radius, and in the same time, uniformly round O.

Hence the acceleration of P is made up of a constant acceleration in the direction CP, and of an equal constant acceleration in the direction CO. Therefore its whole acceleration will be represented in magnitude and direction by OP; or tends to O, and varies as the distance from O.

Note. If the point P be fixed relatively to, though not on the circumference of the moving circle, it may be proved in a similar manner that its acceleration will still tend to O, and be proportional to OP. In this case, it may be geometrically proved that the path of P will be an ellipse of which O is the centre; hence we learn that if the acceleration of a moving point tend to a fixed point, and vary as the distance from it, its path will be an ellipse of which the fixed point is the centre; the converse of Newton, Sect. II. Prop. 9.

iv. Prove that, when a body moves along a smooth tube under the action of any force tending to a point and varying as the distance from the point, the difference of the squares of the velocities at the beginning and end of an arc varies as the difference of the squares of the distances of the extremities of the arc from the fixed point.

The acceleration in $PQ = \mu \cdot SP \cdot \dfrac{Pm}{PQ}$, ultimately, fig. 32;

$\therefore$ (vel.)^2 at Q — (vel.)^2 at $P = 2\mu SP \cdot \dfrac{Pm}{PQ} \cdot PQ$

$= 2\mu SP \cdot Pm$, ultimately,

$= \mu (SP + SQ)(SP - SQ)$

$= \mu (SP^2 - SQ^2)$, ultimately;

$\therefore$ by Lemma IV.

(vel.)^2 at SA — (vel.)^2 at $B = \mu (SA^2 - SB^2)$.

v. A body is revolving in an ellipse under the action of such a force, and when it arrives at the extremity of the major axis the force ceases to act until the body has moved through a distance equal to the semi-minor axis, it then acts for a quarter of the periodic time in the ellipse; prove that, if it again ceases to act for the same time as before, the body will have arrived at the other extremity of the major axis.

The velocity at $A = \sqrt{\mu} CB =$ velocity at D. Fig. 33.

The body on arriving at D proceeds to describe an ellipse of which CD and CS are semi-conjugate diameters, and in a quarter of the periodic time it arrives at B and moves with velocity $\sqrt{\mu} CD$ in direction parallel to DC and therefore towards a, and arrives at a in time $\dfrac{CD}{\sqrt{\mu} CD} = \dfrac{AD}{\sqrt{\mu} BC}$, the time from A to D.

vi. When a body revolves in an ellipse under the action of a force tending to the focus, find the velocity at any point of its orbit, and the periodic time.

If on arriving at the extremity of the minor axis, the force has its law changed, so that it varies as the distance, the magnitude at that point remaining the same, the periodic time will be unaltered, and the sum of the new axes is to their difference as the sum of the old axes to the distance between the foci.

$$\frac{\mu}{SB^2} = \mu' SB, \quad SB = a;$$

$$\therefore \frac{2\pi}{\sqrt{\mu'}} = \frac{2\pi a^{\frac{3}{2}}}{\sqrt{\mu}},$$

(vel.)^2 at $B = \dfrac{\mu}{a} = \mu' a^2$, where a = semi-diameter parallel to the major axis of the old orbit; if α, β be the semi-axes of the new orbit. Since SB and the semi-conjugate diameter each equals a

$$\alpha^2 + \beta^2 = 2a^2,$$
$$\alpha\beta = ab,$$
$$(\alpha \pm \beta)^2 = 2a(a \pm b);$$
$$\therefore \alpha + \beta : \alpha - \beta :: \sqrt{(a+b)} : \sqrt{(a-b)}$$
$$:: a+b : \sqrt{(a^2-b^2)}$$
$$:: 2(AC+BC) : SH.$$

MONDAY, *Jan.* 16. 9 *to* 12.

SENIOR MODERATOR. Arabic numbers.
SENIOR EXAMINER. Roman numbers.

1. A UNIFORM heavy ellipsoid has a given point in contact with a smooth horizontal plane. Find the plane of the couple necessary to keep it at rest in this position; and investigate its equation referred to the principal axes of the ellipsoid.

The ellipsoid is acted on by its weight vertically downwards, through the centre, and the normal action of the horizontal plane vertically upwards, through the point of contact.

The plane of the required couple must therefore be the vertical plane which passes through the centre and the point of contact or be parallel to this plane. If x, y, z be the co-ordinates of the point of contact referred to the principal axes of the ellipsoid, the equations of the normal at that point are

$$\frac{\xi - x}{\frac{x}{a^2}} = \frac{\eta - y}{\frac{y}{b^2}} = \frac{\zeta - z}{\frac{z}{c^2}}.$$

Hence the plane sought must contain this line, and pass through the centre, or be parallel to the plane thus determined.

Its equation is therefore easily found to be

$$\frac{\xi}{x}\left(\frac{1}{b^2}-\frac{1}{c^2}\right)+\frac{\eta}{y}\left(\frac{1}{c^2}-\frac{1}{a^2}\right)+\frac{y}{z}\left(\frac{1}{a^2}-\frac{1}{b^2}\right)=d,$$

where d is any arbitrary constant.

2. An oblong table has the legs at the four corners alike in all respects, and slightly compressible. Supposing the floor and top of the table to be perfectly rigid, find the pressures on the legs, when the table is loaded in any given manner, supposing the compression to be proportional to the pressure; and prove that, when the resultant weight lies in one of four straight lines on the surface of the table, the table is supported by three legs only.

Let $ABCD$ be the top of the table, the sides AB and AD being $2a$ and $2b$ respectively. See fig. 31.

Let the natural length of each leg be c, and let P be the position of the resultant weight; the co-ordinates of P, referred to AB and AD as axes, being x and y.

Let P_1 P_2 P_3 P_4 be the pressures at the angular points, and let z_1 z_2 z_3 z_4 be the altered lengths of the legs.

Then

$$\frac{c-z_1}{c}=\lambda P, \text{ or } z_1 = c - \lambda c P,$$

and so forth, also neglecting quantities of the second order we shall consider the pressures at the points $ABCD$ to remain vertical;

$$\therefore P_1 + P_2 + P_3 + P_4 = W \dots\dots\dots\dots\dots(1),$$
$$(P_1 + P_4)x - (P_2 + P_3)(2a - x) = 0 \dots\dots\dots(2),$$
$$(P_1 + P_2)y - (P_3 + P_4)(2b - y) = 0 \dots\dots\dots(3),$$

and since the base and top of the table remain rigid, the height of the intersection of its diagonals is

$$\tfrac{1}{2}(z_2 + z_4), \text{ or } \tfrac{1}{2}(z_1 + z_3);$$
$$\therefore z_2 + z_4 = z_1 + z_3;$$
$$\therefore P_2 + P_4 = P_1 + P_3 \dots\dots\dots\dots\dots(4).$$

By elimination between these four equations, we get
$$P_3 = \frac{W}{4} \cdot \left(\frac{x}{a} + \frac{y}{b} - 1\right),$$
with similar values for the other pressures.

If $P_3 = 0$, the weight must lie in the line
$$\frac{x}{a} + \frac{y}{b} - 1,$$
being a line parallel to BD, and bisecting AB and AD.

Hence, when the weight lies in one of four straight lines parallel to the diagonals of the table, the table is supported by three legs only.

3. Find the equations of equilibrium of a perfectly flexible uniform inextensible string when acted on by any given forces.

If a small rough heavy bead be strung upon such a string, and the string be suspended from two points and acted on by gravity only, write down the equations for determining within what portion of the string it is possible for the bead to rest.

Let AP and BP be the two catenaries into which the string is divided when the weight rests in one of its limiting positions of equilibrium as at P. See fig. 32.

Let μ be the coefficient of friction, w the weight of the ring, T and T' the tensions in the two portions of the string, θ and $\theta + \phi$ the inclinations of the tangents at the point P to the horizontal.

The weight cannot affect the horizontal tension, and therefore the parameter c must be the same in both catenaries.

Our equations are therefore
$$T' = T e^{\mu\phi},$$
or $\quad \sec(\theta + \phi) = \sec\theta \, e^{\mu\phi}$ .... (1),
$\quad c\{\tan\theta + \tan(\theta + \phi)\} = w$ .... (2),
$c\sec\alpha - c\sec(\theta + \phi) - c\sec\beta + c\sec\theta = h$ .... (3),
$c\tan\alpha - c\tan(\theta + \phi) + c\tan\beta - c\tan\theta = l$ .... (4),

h and l being the difference in height of A and B, and the length of the string respectively, and α and β the inclinations to the horizon at the points B and A respectively; we have also a fifth geometrical equation indicating that the horizontal distance between A and B is given, and involving no additional unknown quantity. These five equations determine θ, ϕ, α, β, and c, and then BP and AP are known.

iv. A particle is attached by a rod without mass, to the extremity of another rod, n times as long, which revolves in a given manner about the other extremity, the whole motion taking place in a horizontal plane. If θ be the inclination of the rods, ω the angular velocity of the second rod at the time t, prove that

$$\frac{d^2\theta}{dt^2} + \frac{d\omega}{dt} + n\left(\frac{d\omega}{dt}\cos\theta + \omega^2\sin\theta\right) = 0.$$

If a be the length of the rod without weight, na that of the rod whose angular velocity is ω at the time t,

The angular velocity of the particle about the point of junction

$$= \frac{d\theta}{dt} + \omega.$$

The acceleration of the point of junction is

$$na\frac{d\omega}{dt}$$

perpendicular to the rod na and $na\omega^2$ towards the fixed point.

The relative acceleration of the particle perpendicular to the rod a

$$= a\left(\frac{d^2\theta}{dt^2} + \frac{d\omega}{dt}\right);$$

therefore since the whole acceleration in that direction is zero

$$\frac{d^2\theta}{dt^2} + \frac{d\omega}{dt} + n\left(\frac{d\omega}{dt}\cos\theta + \omega^2\sin\theta\right) = 0.$$

v. A bead is capable of free motion on a fine smooth wire in the form of any plane curve, and is acted on by given forces; compare the pressure on the wire with the weight of the bead.

If the wire be a horizontal circle, radius a, and the bead be acted on only by the tension of an elastic string the natural length of which is a, fixed to a point in the plane of the circle at distance $2a$ from its centre, find the condition that the bead may just revolve; and prove that in this case the pressures at the extremities of the diameter through the fixed point will be twice and four times the weight of the bead if that weight be such as to stretch the string to double its natural length.

Let S be the point to which the string is fixed, C the centre of the circle, $SACB$ a straight line meeting the circle in A, B. See fig. 33.

If W be the weight of the particle, r the length of the string, a the radius of the circle,

$$\text{the tension} = W \cdot \frac{r-a}{a},$$

$$\text{and its accelerating effect} = g \cdot \frac{r-a}{a}.$$

If v be the velocity of the particle when the length of the string is r, u, v the velocities at B and A,

$$v^2 - u^2 = -2g \int_a^r \frac{r-a}{a} dr;$$

$$\therefore u^2 - v^2 = g \frac{(r-a)^2}{a};$$

$$\therefore u^2 = 4ag.$$

Pressure at A is that due to the acceleration $\dfrac{u^2}{a}$

$$= 4W.$$

Pressure on B is the tension of the string at B

$$= 2W.$$

9. A distant circular window is viewed by a short-sighted man through his eye-glass, the axis of which passes

through the centre of the window and is perpendicular to its plane. Prove that the image of the window formed by primary focal lines will be spherical, provided the window be filled with concentric rings of stained glass, and the refractive index of the colour throughout any ring be

$$\mu - \frac{(\mu-1)(2\mu+1)}{2\mu} \cdot \frac{r^2}{d^2},$$

μ being the index of the central colour, r the radius of the ring in question, and d the distance of the window from the lens.

When a small pencil of parallel rays passes centrically and with small obliquity (ϕ) through a lens, the distance of the primary focal line from the centre of the lens is

$$f\left\{1 - \left(1 + \frac{1}{2\mu}\right)\phi^2\right\},$$

where $\dfrac{1}{f} = (\mu-1)\left(\dfrac{1}{r} - \dfrac{1}{s}\right)$.

In the case supposed, let f_0 be the focal length for the direct ray and x the refractive index for rays which are incident at the angle ϕ; therefore to satisfy the required condition we must have the following relation between ϕ and x,

$$f\left\{1 - \left(1 + \frac{1}{2x}\right)\phi^2\right\} = f_0;$$

$$\therefore\ 1 - \left(1 + \frac{1}{2x}\right)\phi^2 = \frac{f_0}{f} = \frac{x-1}{\mu-1};$$

$$\therefore\ x - 1 = \mu - 1 - (\mu-1)\left(\frac{2x+1}{2x}\right)\cdot\phi^2,$$

or $\quad x = \mu - \dfrac{(\mu-1)(2\mu+1)}{2\mu}\cdot\dfrac{r^2}{d^2},$

putting μ for x in the coefficient of the small quantity ϕ^2, and substituting $\dfrac{r^2}{d^2}$ as the obvious equivalent of that quantity.

11. Find the parallax in right ascension of a heavenly body, in terms of the latitude of the place of observation, and the hour angle and declination of the body, assuming the distance of the body from the Earth to be so great that the sine and circular measure of the parallax may be considered equal.

Shew that the locus of all the bodies, which on this assumption have their parallaxes in right ascension for a given place and time equal to a given quantity, is a right circular cylinder touching the plane of the meridian of the place along the axis of the heavens.

The parallax in R. A. for bodies satisfying the condition mentioned in the question is

$$\frac{a}{r} \cdot \frac{\cos l \sin h}{\cos \delta},$$

a being the Earth's radius, r the distance of the body, l the latitude of the place, h the hour angle, and δ the declination of the body.

If this be equal to a given quantity m,

$$\frac{a}{r} \cdot \frac{\cos l \sin h}{\cos \delta} = m;$$

or $r^2 \cos^2 \delta = \dfrac{a \cos l}{m} \cdot r \sin h \cos \delta.$

Refer to the plane of the equator as that of xy, the axis of y being perpendicular to the meridian;

$$\therefore x^2 + y^2 = \frac{a \cos l}{m} \cdot y,$$

proving the proposition.

MONDAY, *Jan.* 16.   1½ *to* 4.

JUNIOR MODERATOR.   Arabic numbers.
JUNIOR EXAMINER.   Roman numbers.

1. SHEW how to expand a^x in a series of ascending powers of x.

Prove that the series

$$1 + \frac{2^3}{1.2} + \frac{3^3}{1.2.3} + \frac{4^3}{1.2.3.4} + \ldots = 5e.$$

It may be easily proved by direct multiplication that the series

$$x + \frac{2^3 x^2}{1.2} + \frac{3^3 x^3}{1.2.3} + \ldots = (x^2 + 3x + 1)\, e^x,$$

whence, putting $x = 1$, we have

$$1 + \frac{2^3}{1.2} + \frac{3^3}{1.2.3} + \ldots = 5e.$$

An expression may also be found for the general series

$$1 + \frac{2^n}{1.2} + \frac{3^n}{1.2.3} + \ldots\ldots$$

Since

expanding each term, the required series is easily seen to be the coefficient of t^n in the expansion of ϵ^{e^t}. By Herschel's Theorem this is equal to $\epsilon^{1+\Delta}.0^n$. Hence the required expression is

$$e\left(\Delta 0^n + \frac{\Delta^2 0^n}{1.2} + \frac{\Delta^3 0^n}{1.2.3} + \ldots + \frac{\Delta^{n-1} 0^n}{\lfloor n-1}\right).$$

vi. Find the value of p, in order that the straight line represented by the equation $x\cos\theta + y\sin\theta = p$ may touch the ellipse

$$\frac{x^2}{a^2} + \frac{y^2}{b^2} = 1.$$

Prove that the locus of the vertices of an equilateral triangle described about the ellipse $\frac{x^2}{a^2} + \frac{y^2}{b^2} = 1$ is given by the equation

$$4(b^2 x^2 + a^2 y^2 - a^2 b^2) = 3(x^2 + y^2 - a^2 - b^2)^2.$$

Let x, y be the co-ordinates of one of the vertices of an equilateral triangle described about the ellipse, θ the inclination to the axis of y, of a tangent drawn through it. We have then, for the determination of θ, the equation

$$x\cos\theta + y\sin\theta = (a^2\cos^2\theta + b^2\sin^2\theta)^{\frac{1}{2}},$$

which, rationalized, gives

$$(y^2 - b^2)\tan^2\theta + 2xy\tan\theta + (x^2 - a^2) = 0.$$

If θ_1, θ_2 be the two values of θ given by this equation, we must have, in order that the two tangents represented by it may be inclined at an angle $\frac{\pi}{3}$,

$$\tan(\theta_1 - \theta_2) = \tan\frac{\pi}{3} = \sqrt{3},$$

that is,

$$\frac{\tan\theta_1 - \tan\theta_2}{1 + \tan\theta_1 . \tan\theta_2} = \sqrt{3}.$$

Now

$$\tan\theta_1 + \tan\theta_2 = -\frac{2xy}{y^2 - b^2},$$

$$\tan\theta_1 \tan\theta_2 = \frac{x^2-a^2}{y^2-b^2};$$

$$\therefore \frac{\left(\dfrac{2xy}{y^2-b^2}\right)^2 - b\,\dfrac{x^2-a^2}{y^2-b^2}}{\left(1+\dfrac{x^2-a^2}{y^2-b^2}\right)^2} = 3;$$

$$\therefore \frac{4x^2y^2 - 4(x^2-a^2)(y^2-b^2)}{(x^2+y^2-a^2-b^2)^2} = 3,$$

or $3(x^2+y^2-a^2-b^2)^2 = 4(b^2x^2+a^2y^2-a^2b^2)$,

a relation between x and y, which gives the required locus*.

8. Prove that, if a straight line be drawn from the origin to cut the straight line $\dfrac{x-a}{l} = \dfrac{y-b}{m} = \dfrac{z-c}{n}$ at right angles, its equations will be

$$\frac{x}{a-lt} = \frac{y}{b-mt} = \frac{z}{c-nt},$$

where
$$t = \frac{al+bm+cn}{l^2+m^2+n^2}.$$

Let the given line be

$$\frac{x-a}{l} = \frac{y-b}{m} = \frac{z-c}{n} = -t,$$

and the required line

$$\frac{x}{\lambda} = \frac{y}{\mu} = \frac{z}{\nu}.$$

Then, since these must intersect and also be at right angles, we have

$$\left.\begin{array}{c} \dfrac{a-lt}{\lambda} = \dfrac{b-mt}{\mu} = \dfrac{c-nt}{\nu}, \\ l\lambda + m\mu + n\nu = 0, \end{array}\right\}$$

---

* It will be observed that this curve consists of two closed portions, one wholly within the other. The outer one alone satisfies the condition of the question. The inner is the locus of the intersection of tangents, inclined to one another at an angle $\dfrac{2\pi}{3}$.

whence
$$t = \frac{al + bm + cn}{l^2 + m^2 + n^2},$$

and the ratios $\lambda : \mu : \nu$ are found.

9. If α, β, γ be the distances of a point from the three faces of a tetrahedron which meet in the vertex, prove that the equation of the plane passing through the vertex, and through the centres of the circles inscribed in and circumscribed about the base, is

$$(\cos B - \cos C)\, p_1 \alpha + (\cos C - \cos A)\, p_2 \beta$$
$$+ (\cos A - \cos B)\, p_3 \gamma = 0,$$

where A, B, C are the angles of the base, and p_1, p_2, p_3 the perpendiculars from the vertex on the sides of the base.

Let the equation to the required plane be

$$L\alpha + M\beta + N\gamma = 0.$$

Let r = radius of inscribed circles and let $(\alpha\delta)$, $(\beta\delta)$, $(\gamma\delta)$ be the angles made by the three faces $\alpha\beta\gamma$ with the third face δ, then $\alpha = r\sin(\alpha\delta)$, $\beta = r\sin(\beta\delta)$, $\gamma = r\sin(\gamma\delta)$ must satisfy this equation;

$$\therefore L\sin(\alpha\delta) + M\sin(\beta\delta) + N\sin(\gamma\delta) = 0.$$

But the volume of the pyramid $= \tfrac{1}{3} p \sin(\gamma\delta)$, area of base δ, with two similar expressions. Therefore substituting for $\sin(\gamma\delta)$, $\sin(\beta\delta)$, $\sin(\alpha\delta)$, we get

$$\frac{L}{p} + \frac{M}{p'} + \frac{N}{p''} = 0.$$

Again, if R = radius of circumscribing circle, then

$$\alpha = R \cos A \sin(\alpha\delta),$$

and two similar expressions for β and γ must satisfy the equation;

$$\therefore \frac{L\cos A}{p} + \frac{M\cos B}{p'} + \frac{N\cos C}{p''} = 0.$$

Hence by cross multiplication we find

$$\frac{L}{(\cos B - \cos C)\,p} = \frac{M}{(\cos C - \cos A)\,p'} = \frac{N}{(\cos A - \cos B)\,p''}.$$

10. Find the equation of the sphere, passing through a given point and through the circle in which the polar plane of that point with respect to a given sphere cuts that sphere.

Let the equation to the given sphere be

$$x^2 + y^2 + z^2 = a^2,$$

and the co-ordinates of the given point g, h, k; then the equation to the plane of contact is

$$gx + hy + kz = a^2;$$

and the equation to every sphere passing through the intersection of these two is included in

$$x^2 + y^2 + z^2 - a^2 - \lambda\,(gx + hy + kz - a^2) = 0.$$

But by the question, this goes through $x = g$, $y = h$, $z = k$. Hence by substitution $\lambda = 1$, and the required sphere is

$$x^2 + y^2 + z^2 = gx + hy + kz.$$

11. If a sphere touch an ellipsoid and also cut it, the common section cannot be a plane curve unless the point of contact be one of four fixed points on the ellipsoid.

When two surfaces of the second degree intersect, if one intersection be a plane curve, the other is plane also. Hence, as all the plane sections of a sphere are circles if a sphere cut an ellipsoid in a plane curve, both that curve and the other intersection must be circular sections. Hence in the limit when the sphere touches the ellipsoid, it must touch it at the four umbilici or the points which are the evanescent circular sections.

TUESDAY, *Jan.* 17. 9 *to* 12.

SENIOR MODERATOR. Arabic numbers.
JUNIOR MODERATOR. Roman numbers.

i. FIND a point the distances of which from three given points, not in the same straight line, are proportional to p, q, and r respectively, the four points being in the same plane.

Let A, B and C be the three points.

Divide AB in D so that $AD : DB :: p : q$, and in AB produced take a point E such that
$$AE : BE :: p : q;$$
upon DE, as diameter, describe a circle.

Every point upon this circle has its distances from A and B proportional to p and q respectively.

Describe a similar circle relative to A and C.

The points of intersection of these circles, when intersection is possible, satisfy the required condition.

2. If TP, TQ be two tangents drawn from any point T to touch a conic in P and Q, and if S and H be the foci, then
$$\frac{ST^2}{SP \cdot SQ} = \frac{HT^2}{HP \cdot HQ}.$$

The construction of the figure being indicated by the question, we have, see fig. 34,

$$\frac{SP}{ST} = \frac{\sin STP}{\sin SPT}, \quad \frac{SQ}{ST} = \frac{\sin STQ}{\sin SQT};$$

$$\therefore \frac{SP.SQ}{ST'^2} = \frac{\sin STP . \sin STQ}{\sin SPT . \sin SQT}.$$

Similarly $\quad \dfrac{HP.HQ}{HT'^2} = \dfrac{\sin HTP . \sin HTQ}{\sin HPT . \sin HQT}.$

Now these angles STP, HTQ are known to be equal; and the angles SPT, HPT are supplements, and also the angles SQT, HQT. Hence the above two expressions are equal, and hence

$$\frac{SP.SQ}{ST^2} = \frac{HP.HQ}{HT^2}.$$

If the conic become a parabola, these expressions become each equal to unity.

iii. A polygon is inscribed in an ellipse so that each side subtends the same angle at one of the foci. Prove that, if the alternate sides be produced to meet, their points of intersection will lie on a conic section having the same focus and directrix as the original ellipse, and that the chords joining the consecutive points of intersection all subtend the same constant angle at the focus as the sides of the original polygon.

The polar equation of a chord of an ellipse, the focus being the pole and the line to the nearer vertex the prime radius, is

$$\frac{l}{r} = e \cos \theta + \sec \beta \cos (\alpha - \theta),$$

2β being the angle subtended by the chord at the focus, and $\alpha - \beta$, $\alpha + \beta$ the angles corresponding to its extremities.

If this be taken as the equation of one of the produced sides of the polygon in question, then the side which intersects it has for its equation

$$\frac{l}{r} = e \cos \theta + \sec \beta \cos (\alpha + 4\beta - \theta);$$

therefore at the point of intersection
$$\cos(\alpha - \theta) = \cos(\alpha + 4\beta - \theta),$$
$$\alpha + 4\beta - \theta = \theta - \alpha,$$
$$\theta = \alpha + 2\beta,$$
$$\alpha = \theta - 2\beta,$$
$$\frac{l}{r} = e\cos\theta + \sec\beta \cos 2\beta,$$
$$\frac{l}{\sec\beta \cos 2\beta} \cdot \frac{1}{r} = \frac{e \cos\theta}{\sec\beta \cos 2\beta} + 1,$$

the equation to a conic section having the same focus as the ellipse, but latus rectum and eccentricity each altered in the ratio of $1 : \sec\beta \cos 2\beta$.

Hence the directrix is the same as before.

Also since
$$\theta = \alpha + 2\beta,$$
it follows that the line joining the focus with the point of intersection of any two alternate sides bisects the angle subtended by the intermediate side, and therefore the sides of the new polygon each subtend the angle 2β at the focus.

This proposition may be also solved in an obvious manner by the method of reciprocal polars.

4. Prove that the equiangular spiral is the only curve such that its radius of curvature is proportional to the reciprocal of the radius of curvature at the corresponding point of the reciprocal polar.

Let PY be the tangent to one curve, QZ the tangent to the corresponding point of the reciprocal polar. See fig. 35. Let $OP = r$, $OY = p$, and $OQ = r'OZ = p'$. Then $p'r = \kappa^2$, $pr' = \kappa^2$, where κ is some constant. Also if $\rho\rho'$ be the two radii of curvature at P, Q,

$$\rho' = r'\frac{dr'}{dp'} = \frac{\kappa^2}{p} \cdot \frac{d\left(\frac{\kappa^2}{p}\right)}{d\left(\frac{\kappa^2}{r}\right)} = \frac{\kappa^2 r^2}{p^3} \cdot \frac{dp}{dr} = \frac{\kappa^2 r^2}{p^3} \cdot \frac{1}{\rho}.$$

Hence by the question $\dfrac{\kappa^2 r^3}{p^3}$ = constant, but $\dfrac{p}{r}$ = sin OPY; therefore the angle OPY = constant, or the curve is the equiangular spiral.

5. If two plane sections of a right cone be taken, having the same directrix, the foci corresponding to that directrix lie on a straight line which passes through the vertex.

Let ABC be the given cone; and a perpendicular through L to the plane of the paper the given latus rectum. Fig. 36.

Draw LCB perpendicular to the axis of the cone, and describe a sphere touching the cone in B and C; draw LP, LQ tangents to the sphere in the plane of the paper, we know that P and Q are the foci of the two sections.

Now PQ is the polar line of L, and BCL the polar line of A. Because the pole of PQ lies on BCL therefore the pole of PQ, therefore PQ, passes through A.

vi. Find the equation of the envelope of the perpendiculars to the successive focal radii of a parabola drawn through the extremities of these radii.

Refer to polar co-ordinates, the focus S being the pole and AS the prime radius.

If AQ be a radius vector to the parabola perpendicular to which any line is drawn, and if AQ be inclined at the angle ϕ to AS, its length being p, we have

$$p = a \sec^2 \dfrac{\phi}{2},$$

if θ and r be the polar co-ordinates of the point where the line perpendicular to AQ is intersected by its consecutive, we have

$$r = p \sec(\theta - \phi) = a \sec^2 \dfrac{\phi}{2} \sec(\theta - \phi),$$

or

$$\dfrac{a}{r} = \cos^2 \dfrac{\phi}{2} \cos(\theta - \phi),$$

and $\quad 0 = -\cos\dfrac{\phi}{2}\sin\dfrac{\phi}{2}\cos(\theta-\phi) + \cos^2\dfrac{\phi}{2}\sin(\theta-\phi)$

$\qquad = \cos\dfrac{\phi}{2}\sin(\theta-\phi) = \sin\dfrac{\phi}{2}\cos(\theta-\phi);$

$$\therefore \sin\left(\theta - 3\dfrac{\phi}{2}\right) = 0;\ \therefore\ \phi = \dfrac{2}{3}.\theta;$$

$$\therefore\ \theta - \phi = \dfrac{1}{3}\theta;$$

$$\therefore\ \dfrac{a}{r} = \cos^3\dfrac{\theta}{3};$$

$$\therefore\ r = a\sec^3\dfrac{\theta}{3},$$

the equation required.

vii. If two concentric rectangular hyperbolas have a common tangent, the lines joining their points of intersection to their respective points of contact with the common tangent will subtend equal angles at their common centre.

Let O be the common centre.

Let OX and OY be the asymptotes of one hyperbola,

OX' ... OY' .... the other.

Let $XOX' = 2\alpha$, and let the line OC which bisects this angle be taken as the prime radius.

Let $r\cos(\theta - \beta) = b$ be the equation of the common tangent, b being the perpendicular upon it from the centre, and β the angle between this perpendicular and the prime radius.

Then if P and P' be the respective points of contact of this tangent with the hyperbolas, it follows from the geometry of the hyperbola that

$$COP = -(2\alpha + \beta),$$

and $\qquad COP' = (2\alpha - \beta).$

Now the equations of the hyperbolas are

$$r^2\cos 2(\theta + \alpha) = a^2,$$

$$r^2\cos 2(\theta - \alpha) = a_1^2,$$

and combining these with $r \cos (\theta - \beta) = b$, or the equation of the common tangent, we obtain

$$OP^2 \cos 2(\alpha + \beta) = a^2,$$
$$OP^2 \cos^2 2(\alpha + \beta) = b^2;$$

therefore $\qquad \cos 2(\alpha + \beta) = \dfrac{b^2}{a^2},$

and similarly $\qquad \cos 2(\alpha - \beta) = \dfrac{b^2}{a_1^2}.$

Also if θ_1 be the value of θ corresponding to Q, the point of intersection of the two hyperbolas, we obtain

$$\frac{\cos 2(\theta_1 + \alpha)}{a^2} = \frac{\cos 2(\theta_1 - \alpha)}{a_1^2};$$

therefore $\qquad \dfrac{\cos 2(\theta_1 + \alpha)}{\cos 2(\theta_1 - \alpha)} = \dfrac{a^2}{a_1^2} = \dfrac{\cos 2(\alpha - \beta)}{\cos 2(\alpha + \beta)},$

whence we obtain $\qquad \tan 2\theta_1 = -\tan 2\beta),$

and hence $\qquad POQ = 2\alpha = P'OQ.$

viii. If P be a point on a geodesic line AP, drawn on a conoidal surface, s the length of AP, σ, N, and O the projections of s, P, and the axis on any plane perpendicular to the axis, and p the projection of ON on the tangent to AP at P, then

$$\frac{dp}{d\sigma} = \frac{d\sigma}{ds}.$$

Since the geodesic line on any surface satisfies the condition that its osculating plane at any point contains the normal to the surface at that point, we have for its differential equations

$$\frac{d^2x}{ds^2} + \frac{dz}{dx}\frac{d^2z}{ds^2} = 0,$$
$$\frac{d^2y}{ds^2} + \frac{dz}{dy}\frac{d^2z}{ds^2} = 0;$$

$$\therefore \; x\frac{d^2x}{ds^2} + y\frac{d^2y}{ds^2} + \frac{d^2z}{ds^2}\left(x\frac{dz}{dx} + y\frac{dz}{dy}\right) = 0.$$

In a conoidal surface if the axis coincide with the axis of z,

$$x\frac{dz}{dx} + y\frac{dz}{dy} = 0;$$

$$\therefore x\frac{d^2x}{ds^2} + y\frac{d^2y}{ds^2} = 0,$$

or $\dfrac{d}{ds}\cdot\left(x\dfrac{dx}{ds} + y\dfrac{dy}{ds}\right) = \left(\dfrac{dx}{ds}\right)^2 + \left(\dfrac{dy}{ds}\right)^2.$

But $x\dfrac{dx}{ds} + y\dfrac{dy}{ds} = $ the quantity denoted by p in the question, and

$$\left(\frac{dx}{ds}\right)^2 + \left(\frac{dy}{ds}\right)^2 = \left(\frac{d\sigma}{ds}\right)^2;$$

$$\therefore \frac{dp}{ds} = \left(\frac{d\sigma}{ds}\right)^2,$$

$$\frac{dp}{d\sigma} = \frac{d\sigma}{ds}.$$

9. A string is placed on a smooth plane curve under the action of a central force F, tending to a point in the same plane; prove that, if the curve be such that a particle could freely describe it under the action of that force, the pressure of the string on the curve referred to a unit of length will be

$$= \frac{F\sin\phi}{2} + \frac{c}{\rho},$$

where ϕ is the angle which the radius vector from the centre of force makes with the tangent, ρ is the radius of curvature, and c is an arbitrary constant.

If the curve be an equiangular spiral with the centre of force in the pole, and if one end of the string rest freely on the spiral at a distance a from the pole, then the pressure is equal to

$$\frac{\mu\sin\phi}{2r}\left(\frac{1}{r^2} + \frac{1}{a^2}\right).$$

Let T be the tension at any point, R the pressure referred to a unit of area, then by the ordinary equations for the equilibrium of a string

$$\left. \begin{array}{r} \dfrac{dT}{ds} = F\cos\phi, \\ \dfrac{T}{\rho} + F\sin\phi = R; \end{array} \right\}$$

$$\therefore R = F\sin\phi + \frac{\int F\cos\phi\, ds}{\rho} \quad\ldots\ldots\ldots\ldots (1).$$

Let $v =$ velocity of the particle freely describing the curve, then

$$\left. \begin{array}{r} \dfrac{dv^2}{ds} = -2F'\cos\phi, \\ \dfrac{v^2}{\rho} = F\sin\phi; \end{array} \right\}$$

$$\therefore 0 = \frac{F\sin\phi}{2} + \frac{\int F\cos\phi\, ds - c}{\rho} \quad\ldots\ldots\ldots (2).$$

Subtracting (2) from (1),

$$R = \frac{F\sin\phi}{2} + \frac{c}{\rho}$$

$$= \tfrac{1}{2}\text{ normal force} + \frac{c}{\rho}.$$

The quantity c depends on the tightness with which the string is tied. If one end be free it is to be determined from the condition that $T = 0$ at that end.

If the curve be an equiangular spiral, ϕ is constant and $F = \dfrac{\mu}{r^3}$. Also from (2)

$$0 = \frac{F\sin\phi}{2} + \frac{T - c}{\rho};$$

therefore when $r = a$, and $\rho\sin\phi = r$, we have

$$0 = \frac{\mu\sin\phi}{2a^3} - \frac{c\sin\phi}{a};$$

$$\therefore R = \frac{\mu \sin \phi}{2r} \cdot \left(\frac{1}{r^2} + \frac{1}{a^2}\right).$$

10. If a string, the particles of which repel each other with a force varying as the distance, be in equilibrium when fastened to two fixed points, prove that the tension at any point varies as the square root of the radius of curvature.

The law of attraction being as the distance, the attraction of the whole arc on any particle is the same as if the whole mass was collected at its centre of gravity. Take this point for origin, and let T be the tension at any point whose radius vector is r, let p be the perpendicular on the tangent and ρ the radius vector. Then the equations of equilibrium will be

$$\left. \begin{array}{l} dT = -\mu r dr, \\ Tp = c; \end{array} \right\}$$

$$\therefore \frac{c}{p} = c' - \frac{\mu r^2}{2};$$

$$\therefore -\frac{1}{p^2} = -\mu r \frac{dr}{dp};$$

$$\therefore \rho \propto \frac{1}{p^2};$$

$$\therefore T \propto \frac{1}{p} \propto \sqrt{\rho}.$$

11. If any uniform arc of an equiangular spiral attract a particle, placed at the pole with a force varying inversely as the square of the distance, prove that the resultant attraction acts along the line joining the pole with the intersection of the tangents at the extremities of the arc.

Prove also that, if any other given curve possess this same property, the law of attraction must be $F = \frac{\mu}{p^2} \frac{dp}{dr}$, where p is the perpendicular drawn from the attracted particle on the tangent at the point of which the radius vector is r.

It may be easily proved, if a string be in equilibrium in the form of an equiangular spiral under the action of a force in the pole, that the force must vary as $\dfrac{1}{(\text{dist.})^2}$. And the resultant repulsion of the centre of force on the string, being in equilibrium with the tensions at the extremities, must pass through the intersection of the tangents at the extremities of the arc. Now let the arc become a rigid wire attracting the pole, then all the forces are unaltered, and therefore their resultant, just as before, acts along the line joining the pole with the intersection of the tangents at the extremities of the arc.

In the same way, if any other curve possesses this property, the law of attraction must be such that a string may rest in equilibrium under a centre of force whose law of repulsion is the same. By writing down the equations of equilibrium it is easily seen that this must be the law

$$F = \frac{\mu}{p^2} \frac{dp}{dr}.$$

xii. A material particle is acted on by a force the direction of which always meets an infinite straight line AB at right angles, and the intensity of which is inversely proportional to the cube of the distance of the particle from the line. The particle is projected with the velocity from infinity from a point P at a distance a from the nearest point O of the line in a direction perpendicular to OP, and inclined at the angle α to the plane AOP. Prove that the particle is always on the sphere of which O is the centre, that it meets every meridian line through AB at the angle α, and that it reaches the line AB in the time

$$\frac{a^2}{\sqrt{\mu}\cos\alpha},$$

μ being the absolute force.

Suppose first that the particle is constrained to move in contact with the smooth surface of the sphere mentioned in the question. Then if r be the distance of the particle from the attracting line at any instant, and ϕ the azimuth of the plane containing r, we have, by taking moments round the axis,

$$r^2 \frac{d\phi}{dt} = C.$$

Also if v be the corresponding velocity of the particle, we have

$$v^2 = C' - 2\int \frac{\mu}{r^3} dr = \frac{\mu}{r^2} + C' = \frac{\mu}{r^2}.$$

Since the velocity is that from infinity and therefore $C' = 0$,

$$\therefore r\frac{d\phi}{dt} = \frac{C}{\sqrt{\mu}} \cdot v.$$

But $r\dfrac{d\phi}{dt}$ is the resolved part of the whole velocity perpendicular to the meridian. Hence it follows that the path on the sphere is always inclined to the meridian at an angle whose sine is $\dfrac{C}{\sqrt{\mu}}$; therefore if θ be the angular distance of the particle from the pole of the attracting line,

$$a\frac{d\theta}{dt} = -v\cos\alpha = -\frac{\sqrt{\mu}}{r}\cos\alpha;$$

$$\therefore \frac{dt}{d\theta} = -\frac{ar}{\sqrt{\mu}\cdot\cos\alpha} = -\frac{a^2\sin\theta}{\sqrt{\mu}\cdot\cos\alpha};$$

$$\therefore t = \frac{a^2}{\sqrt{\mu}\cos\alpha}\int_0^{\frac{\pi}{2}} \sin\theta\, d\theta = \frac{a^2}{\sqrt{\mu}\cos\alpha}.$$

Also the normal pressure = difference between the force resolved along the radius and $\dfrac{\overline{\text{vel.}}|^2}{a}$

$$= \frac{\mu}{r^3}\sin\theta - \frac{\mu}{ar^2} = 0,$$

whence it follows that the particle describes the path mentioned in the question.

13. If a particle slide along a smooth curve which turns with uniform angular velocity ω about a fixed point O, then the velocity of the particle relatively to the moving curve is given by the equation

$$v^2 = c^2 + \omega^2 r^2,$$

where r is the distance of the particle from the point O; and the pressure on the curve will be given by the formula

$$\frac{R}{m} = \frac{v^2}{\rho} + \omega^2 p + 2\omega v,$$

where m is the mass of the particle, and p the perpendicular from O on the tangent.

Take $ox\ oy$ axes moving with the curve, and let R be the reaction at any point. Then we have the equations

$$\left. \begin{aligned} \frac{d^2x}{dt^2} - \omega^2 x - \frac{1}{y}\frac{d}{dt}(\omega y^2) &= \frac{R}{m}\frac{dy}{ds}, \\ \frac{d^2y}{dt^2} - \omega^2 y + \frac{1}{x}\frac{d}{dt}(\omega x^2) &= -\frac{R}{m}\frac{dx}{ds}. \end{aligned} \right\}$$

If ω be constant, as given in the question, these equations become

$$\left. \begin{aligned} \frac{d^2x}{dt^2} &= \omega^2 x + \left(\frac{R}{m} + 2\omega v\right)\frac{dy}{ds}, \\ \frac{d^2y}{dt^2} &= \omega^2 y - \left(\frac{R}{m} + 2\omega v\right)\frac{dx}{ds}, \end{aligned} \right\}$$

where $v =$ velocity of the particle relative to the curve.

From these equations we infer that the motion relative to the curve is the same as if the curve was fixed, and a repulsive force $\omega^2 r$ acted from O. Hence, resolving along the tangent,

$$v\frac{dv}{ds} = \omega^2 r \frac{dr}{ds};$$

$$\therefore v^2 = c + \omega^2 r^2.$$

Also the pressure will be $\dfrac{R}{m} + 2\omega v$. Resolving along the normal, we get

$$\frac{v^2}{\rho} = -\omega^2 r \sin\phi - \left(\frac{R}{m} + 2\omega v\right);$$

$$\therefore -\frac{R}{m} = \frac{v^2}{\rho} + \omega^2 p + 2\omega v.$$

If ω be not constant, the equation for v cannot be integrated, but the expression for R is

$$-\frac{R}{m} = \frac{v^2}{\rho} + \omega^2 p + 2\omega v + \frac{d\omega}{dt} \cdot \sqrt{(r^2 - p^2)}.$$

14. A string is laid on a smooth table in the form of a catenary, and an impulse is communicated to one extremity in the direction of the tangent, prove (1) that the initial velocity of any point, resolved parallel to the directrix, is proportional to the inverse square of the distance of that point from the directrix, and (2) that the velocity of the centre of gravity of any arc, resolved in the same direction, is proportionally to the angle between the tangents at extremities of the arc directly, and to the length of the arc inversely.

The equation to determine the tension at any point is

$$\frac{d^2 T}{ds^2} - \frac{T}{\rho^2} = 0,$$

or since in the catenary $\rho = \dfrac{c^2 + s^2}{c}$, this becomes

$$\frac{d^2 T}{ds^2} - \frac{c^2}{(c^2 + s^2)^2} T = 0.$$

One integral of this equation we know must be

$$T = my = m\sqrt{(c^2 + s^2)}.$$

Hence, according to rule, assume

$$T = u\sqrt{(c^2 + s^2)};$$

substituting, we get

$$\frac{d^2 u}{ds^2} = -\frac{2s}{c^2 + s^2} \frac{du}{ds},$$

F

$$\therefore u = A \tan^{-1}\frac{s}{c} + B,$$

where A and B are arbitrary constants. Substituting and reducing, we get

$$T = y(A\phi + B),$$

where ϕ is the angle the tangent makes with the directrix, so that $\tan\phi = \frac{s}{c}$.

The velocity resolved in any direction is given by

$$v_x = \frac{d}{ds}(T\cos\phi)$$

$$= \frac{d}{ds}\left(T\frac{c}{y}\right) = Ac\frac{d\phi}{ds}$$

$$= \frac{Ac}{\rho} = \frac{Ac^2}{y^2}.$$

Again, the motion of the centre of gravity of any arc is the same as if all the forces acted directly at that point parallel to their original directions. Hence, if S be the length of any arc, TT' the tensions at the extremities, $\phi\phi'$ the angles those tangents make with the directrix, then the required velocity of the centre of gravity will be given by

$$S.v = T'\cos\phi' - T\cos\phi,$$

$$= CA(\phi' - \phi),$$

whence the proposition follows at once.

XV. A right circular cone floats with its axis horizontal in a fluid, the specific gravity of which is double that of the cone, the vertex of the cone being attached to a fixed point in the surface of the fluid. Prove that for stability of equilibrium the semi-vertical angle of the cone must be less than 60°.

If A be the area of the plane of floatation, h the length of the axis, and a the radius of the base, then if $\delta\theta$ be the angle through which the cone is displaced about an axis through the vertex, perpendicular to the vertical plane through the centre of gravity and the vertex; it follows from Guldinus's properties that the moment tending to turn the body in the opposite direction to the displacement is increased by

$$A\frac{2}{3}h\delta\theta \cdot \frac{3}{4}h, \quad \text{or} \quad \frac{Ah^2}{2}\delta\theta,$$

and diminished by

$$\frac{Va\theta}{\pi}\delta\theta, \quad \text{or} \quad \frac{Aa^2}{6}\delta\theta,$$

(V being the volume of fluid displaced).

Hence the test of stability becomes

$$\frac{a^2}{6} < \frac{h^2}{2},$$

$$\text{or } \frac{a}{h} < \sqrt{3},$$

$$\tan \alpha < \sqrt{3},$$

$$\alpha < 60°;$$

α being the semi-vertical angle of the cone.

xvi. A ribbon of very small uniform thickness h is coiled up tightly into a cylindrical form, and placed with its curved surface in contact with a perfectly rough plane inclined to the horizon at an angle α, the axis of the cylinder being parallel to the intersection of the plane with the horizon. Prove that the time in which the whole will be unrolled is very approximately $\frac{\pi}{4}\sqrt{\left(\frac{6d^2}{gh\sin\alpha}\right)}$, where d is the diameter of the original coil.

We shall consider the section of the coiled up portion of ribbon made by the plane of motion as circular, and neglect the motion of the centre of gravity perpendicular to the inclined plane. The velocity given by these assumptions at any instant is less than the true velocity, and the time thus arrived at for the uncoiling of the whole is greater than the true time, but the error is evanescent except when a finite number of revolutions remain to be made, and the time of unrolling will therefore be very nearly that arrived at on these assumptions, and cannot be greater than such time.

Let r be the radius of the coil at the time t, θ being the angle remaining to be gone through;

$$\therefore \frac{3}{2} r^2 \frac{d^2\theta}{dt^2} = -rg \sin \alpha ;$$

$$\therefore \frac{d^2\theta}{dt^2} = -\frac{2g}{3r} \sin \alpha.$$

Now
$$r = \frac{h}{2\pi} \cdot \theta ;$$

$$\therefore \frac{d^2\theta}{dt^2} = -\frac{4\pi g \sin \alpha}{3h} \cdot \frac{1}{\theta},$$

$$\therefore \left(\frac{d\theta}{dt}\right)^2 = \frac{8\pi g \sin \alpha}{3h} \log \left(\frac{a}{\theta}\right),$$

a being the initial value of θ.

Let
$$\log \left(\frac{a}{\theta}\right) = x^2;$$

$$\therefore \left(\frac{d\theta}{dt}\right)^2 = 4x^2 a^2 e^{-2x^2} \left(\frac{dx}{dt}\right)^2 ;$$

$$\therefore \frac{dt}{dx} = a \sqrt{\left(\frac{3h}{2\pi g \sin \alpha}\right)} e^{-x^2},$$

$$t = a \sqrt{\left(\frac{3h}{2\pi g \sin \alpha}\right)} \int_0^\infty e^{-x^2} dx$$

$$= a \frac{\sqrt{\pi}}{2} \sqrt{\left(\frac{3h}{2\pi g \sin \alpha}\right)}.$$

But
$$\frac{d}{2} = \frac{h}{2\pi} a ;$$

$$\therefore t = \frac{\pi}{4} \sqrt{\left(\frac{6d^2}{gh \sin \alpha}\right)}.$$

17. If three beads, the masses of which are m, m', m'', slide along the sides of a smooth triangle ABC, and attract each other with forces which vary as the distance, find the position of equilibrium. Prove also that, if they be slightly disturbed, the displacement of each will be given by a series of three terms of the form

$$L \sin (nt + \lambda),$$

where L and λ are arbitrary constants, and the values of n are the three positive roots of the equation

$$(n^2 - \alpha)(n^2 - \beta)(n^2 - \gamma) - \cos^2 A\, m'm''(n^2 - \alpha) - \cos^2 B\, m''m\, (n^2 - \beta)$$

$$- \cos^2 C\, mm'\, (n^2 - \gamma) - 2 \cos A \cos B \cos C\, mm'm'' = 0,$$

where α, β, γ represent

$$m'' + m', \quad m + m'', \quad m' + m,$$

respectively.

Let ABC be the triangle, DEF the positions of the three particles. It is obvious that when they are in equilibrium, the perpendiculars to the three sides of the triangle at DEF, must meet in the centre of gravity G of the three masses. Let α, β, γ be the perpendicular distances of G from the three sides. Then taking moments about the perpendicular α, we have

$$m'\beta \sin C = m''\gamma \sin B;$$

$$\therefore \frac{m'\beta}{b} = \frac{m''\gamma}{c} = \frac{m\alpha}{a}.$$

Thus the ratios of α, β, γ are found. Draw BG so that $\dfrac{\sin ABG}{\sin CBG} =$ known ratio $\dfrac{\gamma}{\alpha}$ and draw CG so that $\dfrac{\sin ACG}{\sin BCG} = \dfrac{\beta}{\alpha}$, their intersection G is the required centre of gravity. By drawing the three perpendiculars GD, GE, GF, the positions of m, m', m'' are determined.

To find the time of a small oscillation.

Let x, y, z be the displacements of m, m', m'' from their positions of rest. The attraction of m' on a unit of mass of m, is equivalent to $m'\,ED$ which is equivalent to $m'E'C$ along $E'C$, and $m'CD'$ along CD', where E' and D' are supposed to be the positions of $m'm$ at the moment under consideration. Thus the whole attraction of m' on a unit of mass of m when resolved along BC is

$$m'\,(CD - x) + m'\,(EC - y)\cos C.$$

By treating m'' in the same way we get the equation
$$\frac{d^2x}{dt^2} + (m' + m'')x + m'y\cos C + m''z\cos B = \text{terms independent}$$
of x, y, z.

But when x, y, z all vanish, $\dfrac{d^2x}{dt^2} = 0$, therefore the right-hand side of this equation is zero.

We have also the similar equations

$$\frac{d^2y}{dt^2} + (m'' + m)y + m''z\cos A + mx\cos C = 0,$$

$$\frac{d^2z}{dt^2} + (m + m')z + mx\cos B + m'y\cos A = 0.$$

To solve these, put $x = L\sin nt$, $y = M\sin nt$, $z = N\sin nt$, and we get

$$(m' + m'' - n^2)\,L + m'\cos C\,.\,M + m''\cos B\,.\,N = 0,$$

and two other similar equations. Whence by cross-multiplication the ratios of L, M, N are found to be as the three quantities

$$m'm''\cos A\cos C - m''\cos B\,(m'' + m - n^2),$$

$$m''m\cos B\cos C - m''\cos A\,(m' + m'' - n^2),$$

$$(m' + m'' - n^2)(m'' + m - n^2) - m'm\cos^2 C.$$

Substituting in the last equation we get

$$(n^2 - \alpha)(n^2 - \beta)(n^2 - \gamma) - \cos^2 A\, m'm''(n^2 - \alpha)$$
$$- \cos^2 B\, m''m(n^2 - \beta)$$
$$- \cos^2 C\, m\, m'(n^2 - \gamma) - 2\cos A \cos B \cos C\, m\, m'm'' = 0,$$

where α, β, γ stand for $m' + m''$, $m'' + m$, $m + m'$ respectively.

xviii. The bore of a gun-barrel is formed by the motion of an ellipse of which the centre is in the axis of the barrel, and the plane is perpendicular to that axis, the centre moving along the axis, and the ellipse revolving in its own plane with an angular velocity always bearing the same ratio to the linear velocity of its centre. A spheroidal ball fitting the barrel is fired from the gun. If V be the velocity with which the ball would have emerged from the barrel had there been no twist; prove that the velocity of rotation with which it actually emerges in the case supposed is $\dfrac{2\pi n V}{\sqrt{(l^2 + 4\pi^2 n^2 k^2)}}$, the number of revolutions of the ellipse corresponding to the whole length l of the barrel being n, and k being the radius of gyration of the ball about the axis coinciding with the axis of the barrel, and the gun being supposed to be immovable.

The ball passes along the barrel under the action of a force which is a function of the distance from the breech. If then we assume that there is no friction between the ball and the barrel, the *vis viva* must be the same whether or not there be a twist. If therefore ω and v be the velocities of rotation and translation at emergence in the case supposed, and V the velocity with no twist, we have

$$v^2 + k^2\omega^2 = V^2.$$

But $\quad \dfrac{\omega}{v} = \dfrac{2\pi n}{l}; \quad \therefore v = \dfrac{l}{2\pi n}\omega;$

$$\therefore \omega^2\left(k^2 + \dfrac{l^2}{4\pi^2 n^2}\right) = V^2,$$

$$\omega = \dfrac{2\pi n V}{\sqrt{(l^2 + 4\pi^2 n^2 k^2)}}.$$

xix. An elastic ring of length l, mass m, and elasticity E is placed over the vertex of a smooth cone, the semi-vertical angle of which is α, and stretched upon it to any size. Supposing it then set free, prove that the time before it leaves the cone is

$$\frac{1}{4}\sqrt{\left(\frac{ml}{E}\right)} \cdot \operatorname{cosec} \alpha,$$

the action of gravity being neglected.

Let A be the vertex of the cone, O the centre of the ring at any instant; let $AO = x$, and a be the value of x when the string is unstretched. Fig. 37.

Then an element of the ring whose unstretched length is ds and stretched length $d\sigma$, is acted on by a force $\dfrac{T}{x \tan \alpha} \cdot d\sigma$ along OP, and a force $R d\sigma$ along the normal to the cone.

Now $T = E \cdot \dfrac{x-a}{a}$, therefore if μ be the mass of a unit of length of the unstretched string, we have, resolving along and perpendicular to AP,

$$\mu ds \frac{d^2}{dt^2}\left(\frac{x}{\cos \alpha}\right) = -\frac{T}{x \tan \alpha} \cdot d\sigma \cdot \sin \alpha \quad \ldots\ldots\ldots (1),$$

$$R d\sigma = \frac{T d\sigma}{x \tan \alpha} \cdot \cos \alpha \quad \ldots\ldots\ldots\ldots\ldots\ldots (2);$$

$$\therefore \frac{d^2 x}{dt^2} = -\frac{E}{\mu} \cdot \frac{x-a}{ax} \cdot \frac{d\sigma}{ds} \cdot \cos^2 \alpha.$$

But by similar figures $\dfrac{d\sigma}{ds} = \dfrac{x}{a}$;

$$\therefore \frac{d^2 x}{dt^2} + \frac{E \cos^2 \alpha}{\mu a^2}(x-a) = 0;$$

therefore time before the ring regains its natural length is

$$= \frac{\pi}{2}\sqrt{\left(\frac{\mu a^2}{E \cos^2 \alpha}\right)}$$

$$= \frac{1}{2}\sqrt{\left(\frac{\mu\pi^2 a^2}{E}\right)}\operatorname{cosec}\alpha$$

$$= \frac{1}{2}\sqrt{\left(\frac{\mu 4\pi^2 a^2}{4E}\right)}\operatorname{cosec}\alpha$$

$$= \frac{1}{4}\sqrt{\left(\frac{ml}{E}\right)}\operatorname{cosec}\alpha;$$

and it appears from equation (2) that $R=0$ when $T=0$, that is, when $x=a$ or the string has regained its natural length.

Therefore the ring leaves the cone in the time

$$\frac{1}{4}\sqrt{\left(\frac{ml}{E}\right)}\operatorname{cosec}\alpha.$$

TUESDAY, *Jan.* 17. 1½ *to* 4.

SENIOR EXAMINER. Arabic numbers.
JUNIOR EXAMINER. Roman numbers.

2. IF pq be the image of PQ, placed perpendicular to the axis QCq of a lens or mirror CR, QRq the course of a ray from Q to q, shew that $PQ : pq :: RqC : RQC$.

Hence prove that, with all combinations of lenses for eye-pieces, the magnifying power of a telescope, arranged for parallel or diverging emergent pencils, is the ratio of the diameter of the object-glass or mirror to that of its image formed on emergence from the eye-piece.

If a be the breadth of the object-glass or mirror,

a_1 that of its first image,

$a_2, a_3 \ldots a_{n-1}$ those of the 2nd ... $\overline{n-1}^{\text{th}}$ images,

b those of the last,

ϵ the angle made with the axis by the axis of a pencil incident centrically on the object-glass or mirror,

$\eta_1, \eta_2 \ldots \eta_n$ the angles made by the axis after refraction or reflection at the successive lenses or mirrors, we have, by the proposition,

$$\frac{a}{a_1} = \frac{\eta_1}{\epsilon},$$

$$\frac{a_1}{a_2} = \frac{\eta_2}{\eta_1},$$

....

$$\frac{a_{n-1}}{b} = \frac{\eta_n}{\eta_{n-1}};$$

$$\therefore \frac{a}{b} = \frac{\eta_n}{\epsilon} = \text{magnifying power.}$$

5. Prove that the locus of a point, through which one of the principal axes is in a given direction, is a rectangular hyperbola in the plane of which the centre of gravity lies, and of which one of the asymptotes is in the given direction; unless the given direction be that of one of the principal axes through the centre of gravity.

Let the origin be the centre of gravity and the axis of x the given direction.

(ξ, η, ζ) any position of the point P,

(x, y, z) that of any particle.

Since the line parallel to Ox through P is a principal axis,

$$\Sigma m (x - \xi)(y - \eta) = 0,$$

and $\qquad \Sigma m (x - \xi)(z - \zeta) = 0;$

and since $\quad \Sigma(mx) = 0, \ \Sigma(my) = 0, \text{ and } \Sigma(mz) = 0,$

$$\xi\eta = \frac{\Sigma(mxy)}{\Sigma(m)},$$

$$\xi\zeta = \frac{\Sigma(mxz)}{\Sigma(m)}.$$

If the given direction be that of one of the principal axes through the centre of gravity, the point P lies in the plane of yz or in Ox.

In other cases the locus is a rectangular hyperbola, one of whose asymptotes is in the given direction, and the plane of which has for its equation

$$\frac{\eta}{\Sigma(mxy)} = \frac{\zeta}{\Sigma(mxz)}.$$

WEDNESDAY, Jan. 18. 9 to 12.

SENIOR MODERATOR.

1. A PARABOLA touches one side of a triangle in its middle point and the other two sides produced. Prove that the perpendiculars drawn from the angles of the triangle upon any tangent to the parabola are in harmonical progression.

Let ABC (see fig. 38) be the triangle, and DFE the parabola touching the side BC in its middle point F, and the other two sides produced in D and E respectively.

Then it follows from the geometry of the parabola that AD and AE are bisected in B and C.

Hence if the sides of the triangle opposite B and C be b and c respectively, the equation to the parabola referred to AE and AD as axes is

$$\sqrt{\left(\frac{x}{2b}\right)} + \sqrt{\left(\frac{y}{2c}\right)} = 1,$$

and the equation to the tangent at any point $x'\, y'$ is

$$\frac{x}{\sqrt{(2bx')}} + \frac{y}{\sqrt{(2cy')}} = 1.$$

The perpendiculars upon this tangent from the points A, B, C, the co-ordinates of which are 0,0, 0,c and b,0 respectively, are therefore proportional to

$$1,\ 1 - \sqrt{\left(\frac{c}{2y'}\right)},\ 1 - \sqrt{\left(\frac{b}{2x'}\right)},$$

or $\quad 1, \; \dfrac{1}{2}\left\{1-\sqrt{\left(\dfrac{cx'}{by'}\right)}\right\}, \; \dfrac{1}{2}\left\{\sqrt{\left(\dfrac{by'}{cx'}\right)}-1\right\},$

and $\quad \dfrac{2}{1-\sqrt{\left(\dfrac{cx'}{by'}\right)}}+\dfrac{2}{\sqrt{\left(\dfrac{by'}{cx'}\right)}-1}=\dfrac{2\{\sqrt{(by')}-\sqrt{(cx')}\}}{\sqrt{(by')}-\sqrt{(cx')}}=2,$

whence the proposition is proved.

There is another method of proving this proposition.

By tangential co-ordinates if $\alpha\beta\gamma$ be the perpendicular from ABC upon the tangent to an inscribed conic section, then

$$\dfrac{l}{\alpha}+\dfrac{m}{\beta}+\dfrac{n}{\gamma}=0,$$

l, m, and n being any constants, and the condition that this conic be a parabola is $l+m+n=0$. (Salmon, *Higher Plane Curves*, p. 8, Art. 7.)

If then $l=m=1$, and $n=-2$ we shall have an inscribed parabola, and since in this case

$$\dfrac{1}{\alpha}+\dfrac{1}{\beta}=\dfrac{2}{\gamma},$$

the perpendiculars from the angles upon any tangent are in harmonical progression. Also the form of the tangential equation shews that the parabola bisects one side internally and the other two sides externally in its points of contact with these sides.

2. Find the length of the longest straight line which can be drawn in the interval between two similar, similarly situated and concentric ellipsoids; and, if a line shorter than the line so determined be moved about in the interval, prove that its point of contact with the interior ellipsoid can never lie within the cone represented by the equation

$$\dfrac{x^2}{a^2\{a^2(1-m^2)-r^2\}}+\dfrac{y^2}{b^2\{b^2(1-m^2)-r^2\}}+\dfrac{z^2}{c^2\{c^2(1-m^2)-r^2\}}=0,$$

a, b, c being the semi-axes of the outer ellipsoid, m the ratio of the linear magnitudes of the inner and outer ellipsoid, and $2r$ the length of the line in question, which is assumed greater than $2b \sqrt{(1 - m^2)}$.

What is the meaning of the boundary so determined when $2r$ is less than $2b \sqrt{(1 - m^2)}$ and greater than $2c \sqrt{(1 - m^2)}$?

The longest line must be a tangent to the inner ellipsoid.

Let any tangent be drawn to this ellipsoid, and let r be the parallel central radius of the outer ellipsoid, and let a diameter of length $2a'$ be drawn to the outer ellipsoid passing through the point of contact of the line in question. The segments of this diameter made by the point of contact are $a'(1 - m)$ and $a'(1 + m)$, and therefore if x be the semi-length of the touching line

$$x^2 = \frac{r^2}{a'^2} a'(1 - m) a'(1 + m) = r^2(1 - m^2);$$

therefore any tangent to the inner ellipsoid $= 2r \sqrt{(1 - m^2)}$, where r is the parallel central radius to the outer ellipsoid, and therefore the longest tangent or the line sought

$$= 2a \sqrt{(1 - m^2)}.$$

Again, if a central section be made of the outer ellipsoid by a plane the direction-cosines of the normal to which are l, m, n, the equation for determining the semi-axes of this section is

$$\frac{l^2 a^2}{a^2 - \rho^2} + \frac{m^2 b^2}{b^2 - \rho^2} + \frac{n^2 c^2}{c^2 - \rho^2} = 0 \dots\dots\dots\dots\dots (1),$$

ρ being one of these semi-axes, if then we take ρ such that

$$r = \rho \sqrt{(1 - m^2)},$$

with the restriction $\rho > b$, we shall determine the limiting relation between the direction-cosines of the normal to a plane touching the inner ellipsoid consistent with the *major* axes of the section of the outer ellipsoid made by this plane not being less than $2r$, and therefore the cone formed by lines drawn to the points of contact of such planes will form a boundary within which no point of contact can be situated.

If x, y, z be a point on such a cone

$$\frac{x}{la^2} = \frac{y}{mb^2} = \frac{z}{nc^2} \quad\quad\quad\quad (2),$$

eliminating between (2) and (1), and remembering that

$$\rho^2 = \frac{r^2}{1-m^2},$$

we obtain

$$\frac{x^2}{a^2\{a^2(1-m^2)-r^2\}} + \frac{y^2}{b^2\{b^2(1-m^2)-r^2\}}$$
$$+ \frac{z^2}{c^2\{c^2(1-m^2)-r^2\}} = 0.$$

If $2r$ be $< 2b\sqrt{(1-m^2)}$ and $> 2c\sqrt{(1-m^2)}$, the cone determines a boundary within which if the point of contact be situated the line cannot reach the outer ellipsoid in both extremities, for within this cone the *minor* axes of the sections made by planes of contact will be less than $2r$.

3. If, in a rigid body moving in any manner about a fixed point, a series of points be taken along any straight line in the body, and through these points straight lines be drawn in the direction of the instantaneous motion of the points, prove that the locus of these straight lines is an hyperbolic paraboloid.

Let AB be the line along which the points are taken at any instant, and let $A'B'$ be consecutive positions of the line AB after a very small interval of time dt.

Since the lines the locus of which is required are drawn through the several points of AB in the direction of the respective instantaneous motions of these points, each line must in the limit pass through $A'B'$ as $A'B'$ is brought indefinitely near to AB. Each line also must be parallel to the plane to which the instantaneous axis is perpendicular.

The locus in question is therefore that traced out by a line moving so as to be always parallel to a fixed plane and always to pass through two straight lines.

This locus is the hyperbolic paraboloid.

4. If $f(x, y, z) = 0$ be the equation to a surface, and r be a straight line drawn through the point x, y, z of which the magnitude and direction are any given functions of x, y, z, state what is the relation between the original surface and that whose equation is $n^{r\frac{d}{dr}} f(x, y, z) = 0$, supposing that in the latter equation $x, y,$ and z have been expressed in terms of r and any two other variables independent of r, and that n is a given numerical quantity, and prove that if the two surfaces coincide for all values of n, the line r must lie altogether in either of them.

Apply this to find the partial differential equations of conical and conoidal surfaces respectively when referred to any system of rectangular axes.

Generally the operation $a^{x\frac{d}{dx}} f(x)$ is equivalent to writing ax for x in $f(x)$. See Carmichael's *Calc. Op.* ch. III. sec. 1. If then in $f(x, y, z)$ we replace the variables x, y, z by three others, r, s and t, and then perform the operation

$$n^{r\frac{d}{dr}} f(r, s, t),$$

this is equivalent to writing nr for r in the expression

$$f(r, s, t).$$

Hence the surface determined by the equation

$$n^{r\frac{d}{dr}} f(r, s, t) = 0$$

is such that any line drawn according to the same law as (r) is drawn in the surface

$$f(r, s, t) = 0,$$

is n times as large as in this latter surface.

If these two surfaces be identical for all values of n, it would clearly follow that the line drawn according to this law must lie in either of them, since by keeping s and t constant, but varying r in any manner, we still remain on either surface.

If a, β, γ be the co-ordinates of the vertex of a conical surface, and r the length of the generating line to any point x, y, z on the cone, we have

$$r^2 = (x-a)^2 + (y-\beta)^2 + (z-\gamma)^2;$$

and since by what has just been proved, if $f(x, y, z) = 0$ be the equation to a conical surface, this is identical with the surface

$$n^{r\frac{d}{dr}} f(x, y, z) = 0$$

for all values of (n), it follows that

$$r \frac{d}{dr} f(x, y, z) = 0.$$

But $\quad r\dfrac{d}{dr} = (x-a)\dfrac{d}{dx} + (y-\beta)\dfrac{d}{dy} + (z-\gamma)\dfrac{d}{dz}.$

Hence by substitution we get the partial differential equations of conical surfaces, or

$$(x-a)\frac{df}{dx} + (y-\beta)\frac{df}{dy} + (z-\gamma)\frac{df}{dz} = 0.$$

Again, in conoidal surfaces. If a, β, γ be any point on the axis, l, m, n the direction-cosines of the axis, and r the length of the portion of a generating line drawn from the point x, y, z to the axis; then

$$r^2 = (x-a)^2 + (y-\beta)^2 + (z-\gamma)^2 \\ - \{l(x-a) + m(y-\beta) + n(z-\gamma)\}^2;$$

and since by reasoning similar to the above

$$r\frac{d}{dr} f(x, y, z) = 0,$$

and

$$r\frac{d}{dr} = [(x-a) - l\{l(x-a) + m(y-\beta) + n(z-\gamma)\}]\frac{d}{dx}$$
$$+ [(y-\beta) - m\{l(x-a) + m(y-\beta) + n(z-\gamma)\}]\frac{d}{dy}$$
$$+ [(z-\gamma) - n\{l(x-a) + m(y-\beta) + n(z-\gamma)\}]\frac{d}{dz},$$

we get, putting ρ for $l(x-a) + m(y-\beta) + n(z-\gamma)$,

$$(x-a-l\rho)\frac{df}{dx} + (y-\beta-m\rho)\frac{df}{dy} + (z-\gamma-n\rho)\frac{df}{dz} = 0.$$

5. From a flexible envelope in the form of an oblate spheroid, of which the eccentricity of the generating ellipse is e, the part between two meridians, the planes of which are inclined to each other at the angle $2\pi(1-e)$, is cut away and the edges are then sewed together; prove that the meridian curve of the new envelope will be the curve of sines.

Let $\delta\theta$ be the angle between two consecutive meridians in the original envelope. Let y be the distance of any point P in one of these meridians from the axis of revolution, and s the arc measured up to P from some fixed point on this meridian.

In the new envelope it is clear that if $\delta\theta'$ be the new value of $\delta\theta$, then $\delta\theta' = \dfrac{d\theta}{e}$. Hence if y' be the new value of y, $y' = ey$ and s is unaltered. When these conditions are satisfied the element at P has the same value in both envelopes, since

$$ey \cdot \frac{d\theta}{e} ds = y\, d\theta\, ds,$$

and the old envelope may be developed into the new envelope.

Now in the meridian curve of the oblate spheroid

$$\left(\frac{ds}{dy}\right)^2 = \frac{b^2 - e^2 y^2}{b^2 - y^2};$$

$$\therefore \frac{ds^2}{e^2 dy^2} = \frac{b^2 - e^2 y^2}{e^2 b^2 - e^2 y^2}.$$

Hence, putting ey for y, we have in the new meridian curve

$$\left(\frac{ds}{dy}\right)^2 = \frac{b^2 - y^2}{e^2 b^2 - y^2},$$

and therefore
$$\left(\frac{dx}{dy}\right)^2 = \frac{b^2(1-e^2)}{e^2b^2-y^2};$$

$$\therefore x = b\sqrt{(1-e^2)}\sin^{-1}\frac{y}{eb},$$

or
$$y = eb\sin\frac{x}{b\sqrt{(1-e^2)}},$$

which proves the proposition.

6. If an uniform inextensible and flexible string be stretched over a smooth surface of revolution, prove that the following equations hold:

$$\frac{d}{ds}\left(Tr\frac{dx}{ds}\right) + Xr = 0, \quad\ldots\ldots\ldots\ldots(1),$$

$$\frac{d}{ds}\left(Tr\frac{dy}{ds}\right) - T\frac{dr}{dy} + Yr = 0, \quad\ldots\ldots(2),$$

where ds is the element of the string at any point, dx and dy are corresponding elements of the arc of the circle through that point perpendicular to the meridian, and of the meridian respectively, X and Y are the resolved parts of the impressed forces along these directions, and r is the distance from the axis, the mass of an unit of length of the string being taken as unity. Hence prove that, if such a string be acted upon by a force at all points perpendicular to the axis of revolution, and inversely proportional to the square of the distance from that axis, the string will, if properly suspended, cut every meridian in the same angle.

In the figure (fig. 39), let PQ be an element ds of the string, PN and MQ being the elements dx and dy.

Draw tangents PT and QT to the meridians AP and AQ, meeting the axis produced in O, and let α be the elementary angle between them.

Resolve the forces acting upon the element PQ of the string in the directions PN and PO, by which means the reaction of the smooth surface does not enter into the equations of equilibrium.

The resolved part of the tension at P in direction NP is $T\dfrac{dx}{ds}$ and in direction OP is $T\dfrac{dy}{ds}$.

The resolved part of the tension at Q in direction PN is

$$\frac{d}{ds}\left(T\frac{dx}{ds}\right) - \alpha T\frac{dy}{ds},$$

and in direction PO it is.

$$\frac{d}{ds}\left(T\frac{dy}{ds}\right) + \alpha T\frac{dx}{ds},$$

also the resolved part of the impressed force on the element PQ in direction $PN = Xds$, in direction PO it is Yds.

Hence $\quad\dfrac{d}{ds}\left(T\dfrac{dx}{ds}\right) - \dfrac{\alpha}{ds}T\dfrac{dy}{ds} + X = 0 \ldots\ldots\ldots$ (1),

$\dfrac{d}{ds}\left(T\dfrac{dy}{ds}\right) + \dfrac{\alpha}{ds}T\dfrac{dx}{ds} + Y = 0 \ldots\ldots\ldots$ (2),

also $\quad\alpha = \dfrac{dx}{OP} = \dfrac{dx}{-r\dfrac{dy}{dr}}.$

Substituting, we obtain

$$\frac{d}{ds}\left(T\frac{dx}{ds}\right) + \frac{T}{r}\frac{dx}{ds}\frac{dr}{ds} + X = 0 \ldots\ldots\ldots\ldots (1),$$

$$\frac{d}{ds}\left(T\frac{dy}{ds}\right) - \frac{T}{r}\left(\frac{dx}{ds}\right)^2\frac{dr}{dy} + Y = 0 \ldots\ldots\ldots (2);$$

whence, since

$$\left(\frac{dx}{ds}\right)^2 = 1 - \left(\frac{dy}{ds}\right)^2,$$

we obtain

or
$$\frac{d}{ds}\left(rT\frac{dx}{ds}\right) + Xr = 0, \quad\ldots\ldots\ldots\ldots\ldots\ldots(1),$$

$$\frac{d}{ds}\left(rT\frac{dy}{ds}\right) - T\frac{dr}{dy} + Yr = 0,\ldots\ldots\ldots\ldots\ldots(2),$$

with the law of force assumed in the latter part of the question

$$X = 0, \quad Y = +\frac{\mu}{r^2}\cdot\frac{dr}{dy},$$

multiplying (1) by $\frac{dx}{ds}$, (2) by $\frac{dy}{ds}$, and adding, we get

$$r\frac{dT}{ds} + \frac{\mu}{r}\cdot\frac{dr}{ds} = 0; \quad\therefore\; T = \frac{\mu}{r} + C.$$

If the string be so suspended that $C = 0$,

$$T = \frac{\mu}{r}, \quad\text{or}\; Tr = \mu;$$

and therefore from equation (1) $\frac{dx}{ds}$ = constant, proving the proposition in the question. N.B. Equation (1) might be found at once by taking moments about the axis.

7. A string is wound round a vertical cylinder of radius a in the form of a given helix, the inclination to the horizon being i. The upper end is attached to a fixed point in the cylinder, and the lower, a portion of the string of length $l \sec i$ having been unwound, has a material particle attached to it which is also in contact with a rough horizontal plane, the coefficient of friction being μ. Supposing a horizontal velocity V perpendicular to the free portion of the string to be applied to the particle so as to tend to wind the string on the cylinder, determine the motion; and prove that the particle will leave the plane after the projection of the unwound portion of string upon the plane has described the angle of which the circular measure is

$$\frac{1}{2\mu\tan i}\log\frac{ga}{2\mu V^2\tan^2 i - 2\mu gl\tan i + ga}.$$

In this case, fig. 40, the string coiled round the cylinder remains the same helix throughout the motion, and the particle in contact with the horizontal plane describes the involute of the circular base.

Let PQ be the projection of the unwrapped string at any time t, P being the particle of mass unity, suppose. Let θ be the angle through which PQ has removed from the commencement of motion, and let v be the velocity of P, the tension of the string being T and pressure on the plane R.

Resolving vertically,
$$R = g - T\sin i;$$

horizontally and tangentially,
$$v\frac{dv}{ds} = -\mu R;$$

horizontally and normally,
$$\frac{v^2}{\rho} = T\cos i, \quad PQ = \rho;$$

$$\therefore v\frac{dv}{ds} = -\mu g + \frac{\mu v^2}{\rho}\tan i,$$

or
$$v\frac{dv}{ds} - \mu\frac{v^2}{\rho}\tan i = -\mu g.$$

But $\rho = l - a\theta$, and $ds = (l - a\theta)\,d\theta$;

$$\therefore \frac{v}{l-a\theta}\cdot\frac{dv}{d\theta} - \mu\frac{v^2}{l-a\theta}\tan i = -\mu g;$$

$$\therefore \frac{dv^2}{d\theta} - 2\mu\tan i \cdot v^2 = -2\mu g(l - a\theta);$$

$$\therefore v^2 = Ce^{2\mu\tan i\,\theta} + \frac{g(l-a\theta)}{\tan i} - \frac{ag}{2\mu\tan^2 i};$$

$$V^2 = C + \frac{gl}{\tan i} - \frac{ag}{2\mu\tan^2 i},$$

when the particle leaves the plane

$$v^2 = \frac{g(l-a\theta)}{\tan i};$$

$$\therefore e^{2\mu \tan i \cdot \theta} = \frac{1}{C} \cdot \frac{ag}{2\mu \tan^2 i} = \frac{ag}{2\mu \tan^2 i} \cdot \frac{1}{V^2 - gl \cot i + \frac{ag}{2\mu} \cot^2 i};$$

$$\therefore \theta = \frac{1}{2\mu \tan i} \cdot \log \frac{ag}{2\mu \tan^2 i \, V^2 - 2\mu gl \tan i + ag}.$$

8. A particle is acted on by two centres of force residing in the same point, one attractive, the other repulsive, and varying inversely as the square and cube of the distance respectively. Two consecutive equal apsidal distances are drawn and the portion of the plane of motion included between them is rolled into a right circular cone. Prove that the trajectory described under the circumstances mentioned above becomes a plane curve on the surface of the cone, and that it will be an ellipse, parabola, or hyperbola, according as the velocity in the trajectory was less than, equal to, or greater than that from infinity.

The differential equation of the trajectory on the plane is

$$\frac{d^2u}{d\theta^2} + u\left(1 + \frac{\mu'}{h^2}\right) = \frac{\mu}{h^2} \quad \ldots\ldots\ldots\ldots\ldots (1),$$

μ and μ' being the absolute intensities of the attractive and repulsive forces respectively.

Its polar equation is therefore

$$u = \frac{\mu}{n^2 h^2} + A \cos(n\theta + B) \ldots\ldots\ldots\ldots (2).$$

If $n^2 = 1 + \frac{\mu'}{h^2}$,

The angle between two consecutive equal apsidal distances is $\frac{2\pi}{n}$, and therefore the equation to the projection of the trajectory on the cone made on the plane perpendicular to the cone's axis is

$$\frac{u}{n} = \frac{\mu}{n^2 h^2} + A \cos(\phi + B),$$

or
$$u = \frac{\mu}{nh^2} + nA \cos(\phi + B);$$

since $n = \operatorname{cosec} \alpha$ where α is the semi-vertical angle of the cone, and therefore the cosine of the angle between each generating line and the base of the cone is $\frac{1}{n}$.

This being the equation to a conic section it follows that the trajectory on the cone must be a plane curve, since none but a plane curve on the surface of the cone can be projected into a conic section on the plane perpendicular to the axis. Also the projection, and therefore the original curve, is an ellipse, parabola, or hyperbola, according as

$$A^2 < = > \frac{\mu^2}{n^4 h^4}.$$

Now by (1)
$$v^2 = h^2 \left\{ \left(\frac{du}{d\theta}\right)^2 + u^2 \right\} = 2\mu u - \mu' u^2 + C,$$

and by (2)
$$h^2 \left\{ \left(\frac{du}{d\theta}\right)^2 + u^2 \right\}$$
$$= h^2 u^2 + n^2 h^2 A^2 \sin^2(n\theta + B)$$
$$= n^2 h^2 A^2 - (n^2 - 1) h^2 u^2 + 2\mu u - \frac{\mu^2}{n^2 h^2}$$
$$= n^2 h^2 A^2 - \mu' u^2 + 2\mu u - \frac{\mu^2}{n^2 h^2}.$$

Equating these values of v^2, we obtain
$$n^2 h^2 A^2 - \frac{\mu^2}{n^2 h^2} = C.$$

Hence $\quad A^2 < = > \frac{\mu^2}{n^4 h^4}$, according as
$$C < = > 0,$$

or according as the velocity in the original trajectory was less than, equal to, or greater than that from infinity.

9. A particle is describing an orbit round a centre of force which is any function of the distance, and is acted upon by a disturbing force which is always perpendicular to the plane of the instantaneous orbit and inversely proportional to the distance of the body from the original centre of force. Prove that the plane of the instantaneous orbit revolves uniformly round its instantaneous axis.

Refer the motion of the particle to the following three moveable axes, viz:

The radius vector to the particle,

The tangent to the particle's path,

and The perpendicular to the plane of the instantaneous orbit.

Let $d\theta$ be the elementary angle described by the radius vector in the plane of the orbit in the time dt, and let $d\phi$ be the elementary angle through which the normal to the instantaneous plane has revolved in the same time.

The velocities in the above three directions are respectively

$$\frac{du}{dt}, \quad r\frac{d\theta}{dt}, \quad 0,$$

also in the time dt, the direction in which $\frac{dr}{dt}$ is measured has moved *towards* the direction in which $r\frac{d\theta}{dt}$ is measured through the angle $\frac{d\theta}{dt}dt$, and the direction in which $r\frac{d\theta}{dt}$ is measured has moved from the direction in which $\frac{dr}{dt}$ is measured through the same angle and towards the normal to the instantaneous plane through the angle $\frac{d\phi}{dt}dt$.

If then F be the central force and N the disturbing force,

$$\frac{d^2r}{dt^2} - r\left(\frac{d\theta}{dt}\right)^2 = F \quad \text{...............} (1),$$

$$\frac{1}{r} \cdot \frac{d}{dt}\left(r^2 \frac{d\theta}{dt}\right) = 0 \quad \text{...............} (2),$$

$$r\frac{d\theta}{dt} \cdot \frac{d\phi}{dt} = N \quad \text{...............} (3).$$

But $N = \frac{\mu}{r}$, and from (2) $r^2 \frac{d\theta}{dt} = h$;

$$\therefore \frac{d\phi}{dt} = \frac{\mu}{h} \text{ is constant.}$$

10. A die in the form of a parallelopiped the edges of which are $2a$, $2b$, and $2c$, is loaded in such a manner that the centre of gravity remains coincident with the centre of figure, but the principal moments of inertia about the centre of gravity become equal; if it then fall from any height and without rotation upon a horizontal plane composed of adhesive material so that no point which has once come in contact with the plane can separate from it, prove that the chance of one of the faces bounded by the edges $2b$, $2c$ coming uppermost is

$$\frac{2}{\pi}\sin^{-1}\frac{bc}{\sqrt{\{(a^2 + b^2)(a^2 + c^2)\}}}.$$

Since the principal moments of inertia about the centre of gravity of the die are equal and there is no initial rotation, the die will by the impact of one of its corners upon the horizontal plane acquire a velocity of rotation about an axis perpendicular to the vertical plane through the corner and the centre of gravity. This will continue until an edge through the corner meets the plane. When this takes place, since by the adhesiveness of the plane no point can separate from it, the die must begin to rotate round this edge until a face meets the plane, and on this face the die will rest. Now it follows from the foregoing that the face on which the die will rest is that which was met by the vertical through the centre of gravity when the die first began to descend. To find therefore the chance of the face $2b$, $2c$, lying uppermost we must construct the pyramid, having for vertex the centre of the die and for base the face $2b$, $2c$; and producing its inclined faces to the surface of the sphere of radius unity described about the centre of the die, we must find the area of the spherical quadrilateral whose corners are A, B, C, D, the points in which the lines of intersection of the inclined faces meet the spherical surface. Now the angles of this spherical quadrilateral are equal, and therefore by dividing it into two spherical triangles we obtain for its area

$$4A - 2\pi,$$

or $4\left(A - \dfrac{\pi}{2}\right),$

where A is the mutual inclination of the inclined faces of the pyramid.

Now taking the line through the centre of the die perpendicular to the face $2b$, $2c$, for axis of x, we see that the equations to the inclined faces are

$$bx - az = 0,$$
$$cx - ay = 0,$$

respectively; and therefore the cosine of the angle between them is

$$\pm \frac{bc}{\sqrt{(a^2 + b^2)(a^2 + c^2)}};$$

and taking the negative sign, since the angle sought is obtuse, we have

$$A = \pi - \cos^{-1} \frac{bc}{\sqrt{(a^2 + b^2)(a^2 + c^2)}};$$

and therefore the area sought is

$$4\left\{\frac{\pi}{2} - \cos^{-1} \frac{bc}{\sqrt{(a^2 + b^2)(a^2 + c^2)}}\right\},$$

or $4 \sin^{-1} \dfrac{bc}{\sqrt{(a^2 + b^2)(a^2 + c^2)}},$

the whole surface of the sphere $= 4\pi$.

Hence the chance of either of the required faces lying uppermost is

$$\frac{2}{\pi} \sin^{-1} \frac{bc}{\sqrt{(a^2 + b^2)(a^2 + c^2)}}.$$

11. A uniform sphere is placed in contact with the exterior surface of a perfectly rough cone. Its centre is acted on by a force, the direction of which always meets the axis of the cone at right angles, and the intensity of which varies inversely as the cube of the distance from that axis. Prove that, if the sphere be properly started, the path described by its centre will meet every generating line of the cone on which it lies in the same angle.

The centre of the sphere is always situated on a cone coaxial with and similar to the original cone, the vertex of which is situated in the produced axis of the original cone and at a distance below the vertex of this cone equal to $a \operatorname{cosec} a$ (a being the radius of the sphere). Take this point as origin and refer the position of the sphere's centre to the polar co-ordinates r, ϕ, where ϕ is the angle at which the plane containing the line r and the axis is inclined to a certain fixed plane. Let F be the impressed force on the sphere's centre resolved along this line. It is clear that this is the only part of the impressed force which is not counteracted by the reaction of the cone, and that it $= \dfrac{\mu}{r^3}$.

Let X and Y be the forces of friction along and perpendicular to a generating line, we at once obtain these equations for the motion of the centre of the sphere, assuming its mass to be unity,

$$\frac{d^2 r}{dt^2} - r \sin^2 a \left(\frac{d\phi}{dt}\right)^2 = X - \frac{\mu}{r^3} \quad \ldots\ldots\ldots\ldots\ldots\ldots (1),$$

$$\frac{d}{dt}\left(r^2 \sin a \frac{d\phi}{dt}\right) = Yr \quad \ldots\ldots\ldots\ldots\ldots\ldots (2).$$

Also for the motion of the sphere about its centre let ω_1, ω_2, ω_3 be the instantaneous angular velocities about the three principal axes normal to the cone, parallel to the direction of r, and perpendicular to this direction on the surface of the cone respectively.

Now ω_1 approaches ω_3 with the angular velocity $\dfrac{d\phi}{dt}\cos\alpha$,

ω_2 .... ω_3 .... $\dfrac{d\phi}{dt}\sin\alpha$,

ω_3 recedes from ω_1 with angular velocity $\dfrac{d\phi}{dt}\cos\alpha$, and from ω_2 with the angular velocity $\dfrac{d\phi}{dt}\sin\alpha$.

Hence if A be the moment of inertia of the sphere round a diameter,

$$A\frac{d\omega_1}{dt} - A\omega_3\frac{d\phi}{dt}\cos\alpha = 0 \quad\ldots\ldots\ldots\ldots(3),$$

$$A\frac{d\omega_2}{dt} - A\omega_3\frac{d\phi}{dt}\sin\alpha = -Ya \quad\ldots\ldots\ldots\ldots(4),$$

$$A\frac{d\omega_3}{dt} + A\omega_2\frac{d\phi}{dt}\sin\alpha + A\omega_1\frac{d\phi}{dt}\cos\alpha = Xa \ldots (5).$$

Also $\quad\quad\quad \dfrac{dr}{dt} + a\omega_3 = 0 \quad\ldots\ldots\ldots\ldots(6),$

$$r\sin\alpha\frac{d\phi}{dt} - a\omega_2 = 0 \quad\ldots\ldots\ldots\ldots(7).$$

From (4) and (7)

$$\frac{A}{a}\cdot\frac{d}{dt}\left(r\sin\alpha\frac{d\phi}{dt}\right) + \frac{A}{a}\cdot\frac{dr}{dt}\cdot\frac{d\phi}{dt}\sin\alpha = -Ya,$$

which combined with (2) gives $Y = 0$, and

$$r^2\sin\alpha\frac{d\phi}{dt} = C;$$

$$\therefore \frac{d\phi}{dt} = \frac{C}{r^2\sin\alpha};$$

therefore from (3)

$$\frac{d\omega_1}{dt} + \frac{C}{r^2 a}\frac{dr}{dt}\cot\alpha = 0, \quad \text{or} \quad \omega_1 = \frac{C}{ra}\cot\alpha + C'.$$

Let $C' = 0$, then $\omega_1 = \dfrac{C}{ra}\cot\alpha$;

and also $\omega_2 = \dfrac{r\sin\alpha}{a}\dfrac{d\phi}{dt} = \dfrac{C}{ra}$ from (7).

But the equation of *vis viva* gives us

$$\left(\frac{dr}{dt}\right)^2 + r^2\sin^2\alpha\left(\frac{d\phi}{dt}\right)^2 + A(\omega_1^2 + \omega_2^2 + \omega_3^2) = -2\int\frac{\mu}{r^3}\cdot dr + C''.$$

Substituting for ω_1 and ω_2 and remembering that

$$\omega_3^2 = \frac{1}{a^2}\left(\frac{dr}{dt}\right)^2,$$

and that $\quad r^2\sin^2\alpha\left(\dfrac{d\phi}{dt}\right)^2 = \dfrac{C^2}{r^2},$

we obtain

$$\left(\frac{dr}{dt}\right)^2\left(1 + \frac{A}{a^2}\right) + \frac{C^2}{r^2} + \frac{AC^2\cot^2\alpha}{a^2 r^2} + \frac{AC^2}{r^2 a^2} = \frac{\mu}{r^2} + C''.$$

If now the circumstances of projection be such that $C'' = 0$ as well as C', we obtain

$$\frac{dr}{dt} \propto \frac{1}{r}, \quad \propto r\sin\alpha\frac{d\phi}{dt}.$$

But $\dfrac{dr}{dt}$ and $r\sin\alpha\dfrac{d\phi}{dt}$ are proportional to the velocities of the sphere's centre, parallel and perpendicular respectively to the generating line, drawn to its centre on the cone in which its centre is always situated; hence the proposition is proved.

12. A small rigid vertical cylinder, containing air, is rigidly closed at the bottom, and covered at the top by a disk of very small weight which fits it air-tight. Supposing the

air in the cylinder to be set in vibration, prove that the period of a vibration is $\frac{2\pi}{m}$, m being a root of the equation

$$m \tan \frac{ml}{a} = \frac{\kappa\beta\Pi}{\mu a};$$

where l is the length of the tube, a the velocity of sound in air, μ the mass, κ the area of the disk, $p \propto \rho\,(1+\beta s)$ the relation between the pressure and density when the latter is suddenly changed from ρ to $\rho\,(1+s)$, and Π the pressure of the air on the cylinder before motion commences.

When the disk is first of all placed in the cylinder it sinks through a space which is very small in consequence of the small weight of the disk, and comes to rest when the pressure Π of the air in the cylinder satisfies the condition

$$\Pi = P + \frac{\mu g}{\kappa},$$

P being the pressure of the external air.

The differential equation of the disturbance is

$$\frac{d^2\xi}{dt^2} = a^2 \frac{d^2\xi}{dx^2}.$$

For which we may assume the integral

$$\xi = A \sin m\,(at + x) + A' \sin m\,(at - x).$$

Now measuring x from the bottom of the cylinder we must have the following relations:

(1) When $x = 0$ $\frac{d\xi}{dt} = 0$ for all values of t, whence we readily obtain $A + A' = 0$.

(2) When $x = l$,

$$\mu \frac{d^2\xi}{dt^2} = \Pi\kappa \left(1 - \beta \frac{d\xi}{dx}\right) - P\kappa - \mu g = -\Pi\beta\kappa \frac{d\xi}{dx},$$

because the condensation s at any point is $-\frac{d\xi}{dx}$;

$$\therefore -\mu A m^2 a^2 \{\sin m (at+l) - \sin m (at-l)\}$$
$$= -\Pi\beta\kappa A m \{\cos m (at+l) + \cos m (at-l)\},$$

$$2 \cos mat \sin ml = \frac{\Pi\beta\kappa}{\mu m a^2} 2 \cos mat \cos ml,$$

or
$$m \tan ml = \frac{\Pi\beta\kappa}{\mu a^2};$$

therefore the time of a vibration is

$\frac{2\pi}{ma}$, where m satisfies the equation

$$m \tan ml = \frac{\Pi\beta\kappa}{\mu a^2},$$

or writing m for ma, and therefore $\frac{m}{a}$ for m, this time becomes $\frac{2\pi}{m}$, where m satisfies the equation

$$m \tan \frac{ml}{a} = \frac{\kappa\beta\Pi}{\mu a}.$$

13. A circular drumhead of uniform thickness is stretched with a tension of uniform magnitude at all points in its circumference, and is then set in vibration by a small disturbance commencing at the centre. Prove (1) that if z be the transversal disturbance at the time t of a point the initial distance of which from the centre was r, then

$$\frac{d^2z}{dt^2} = a^2 \left(\frac{1}{r}\frac{dz}{dr} + \frac{d^2z}{dr^2}\right),$$

and (2) that the general primitive of this differential equation is

$$z = \int_0^\pi \phi(at + r\cos\theta) d\theta + \int_0^\pi \psi(at + r\cos\theta) \log(r\sin^2\theta) d\theta,$$

ϕ and ψ being arbitrary functions, and a a constant depending upon the tension and constitution of the drumhead.

The disturbance will be arranged symmetrically about the centre, and we may consider the motion of an elementary annulus, the undisturbed radius of which was r, and its breadth dr.

Let T be the tension of the drumhead, and μ the mass of an unit of area.

The mass of the annulus just referred to is therefore
$$\mu 2\pi r \, dr.$$

The tension along the inner circumference resolved vertically is
$$2\pi r T \frac{dz}{dr},$$
(neglecting the longitudinal displacements) and that along the outer circumference is
$$2\pi r T \frac{dz}{dr} + \frac{d}{dr}\left(2\pi r T \frac{dz}{dr}\right) dr.$$

Hence our equation of disturbance becomes
$$\mu 2\pi r \, dr \cdot \frac{d^2 z}{dt^2} = \frac{d}{dr}\left(2\pi r T \frac{dz}{dr}\right) dr;$$
$$\therefore r \frac{d^2 z}{dt^2} = \frac{T}{\mu} \cdot \frac{d}{dr}\left(r \frac{dz}{dr}\right),$$
T being constant throughout the drumhead;
$$\therefore \frac{d^2 z}{dt^2} = \frac{T}{\mu}\left(\frac{1}{r}\frac{dz}{dr} + \frac{d^2 z}{dr^2}\right).$$

To solve the equation
$$\frac{d^2 z}{dt^2} = a^2 \left(\frac{1}{r}\frac{dz}{dr} + \frac{d^2 z}{dr^2}\right).$$

Assume
$$z = \int_0^\pi \phi\left(at + r\cos\theta\right) d\theta;$$
$$\therefore \frac{dz}{dr} = \int_0^\pi \phi'\left(at + r\cos\theta\right) \cos\theta \, d\theta;$$

and $\dfrac{d^2z}{dt^2} = a^2 \displaystyle\int_0^\pi \phi''(at + r\cos\theta)\, d\theta$;

$\therefore \dfrac{d^2z}{dt^2} - a^2 \dfrac{d^2z}{dr^2} = a^2 \displaystyle\int_0^\pi \phi''(at + r\cos\theta)(1 - \cos^2\theta)\, d\theta$

$\qquad = a^2 \displaystyle\int_0^\pi \phi''(at + r\cos\theta)\sin^2\theta\, d\theta$

$\qquad = -\dfrac{a^2}{r}\displaystyle\int_0^\pi \{\sin\theta\phi'(at + r\cos\theta)\}$

$\qquad\qquad + \dfrac{a^2}{r}\displaystyle\int_0^\pi \phi'(at + r\cos\theta)\cos\theta\, d\theta$

$\qquad = 0 + \dfrac{a^2}{r}\dfrac{dz}{dr}$,

because $\sin\theta = 0$ at both limits.

Again assume

$$z = \int_0^\pi \psi(at + r\cos\theta)\log(r\sin^2\theta)\, d\theta,$$

$\dfrac{dz}{dr} = \displaystyle\int_0^\pi \psi'(at + r\cos\theta)\log(r\sin^2\theta)\cos\theta\, d\theta$

$\qquad + \dfrac{1}{r}\displaystyle\int_0^\pi \psi(at + r\cos\theta)\, d\theta$,

$\dfrac{d^2z}{dr^2} = \displaystyle\int_0^\pi \psi''(at + r\cos\theta)\log(r\sin^2\theta)\cos^2\theta\, d\theta$

$\qquad + \dfrac{2}{r}\displaystyle\int_0^\pi \psi'(at + r\cos\theta)\cos\theta\, d\theta$

$\qquad - \dfrac{1}{r^2}\displaystyle\int_0^\pi \psi(at + r\cos\theta)\, d\theta$,

also

$\dfrac{d^2z}{dt^2} = a^2 \displaystyle\int_0^\pi \psi(at + r\cos\theta)\log(r\sin^2\theta)\, d\theta$;

$$\therefore \frac{d^2z}{dt^2} - a^2 \frac{d^2z}{dr^2} = a^2 \int_0^\pi \psi'' (at + r \cos \theta) \log (r \sin^2 \theta) \sin^2 \theta$$

$$- 2 \frac{a^2}{r} \int_0^\pi \psi' (at + r \cos \theta) \cos \theta d\theta$$

$$+ \frac{a^2}{r^2} \int_0^\pi \psi (at + r \cos \theta) d\theta$$

$$= - \frac{a^2}{r} \int_0^\pi \psi' (at + r \cos \theta) \log (r \sin^2 \theta) \sin \theta$$

$$+ \frac{a^2}{r} \int_0^\pi \psi' (at + r \cos \theta) \log (r \sin^2 \theta) \cos \theta d\theta$$

$$+ 2 \frac{a^2}{r} \int_0^\pi \psi' (at + r \cos \theta) \cos \theta d\theta$$

$$- 2 \frac{a^2}{r} \int_0^\pi \psi' (at + r \cos \theta) \cos d\theta$$

$$+ \frac{a^2}{r^2} \int_0^\pi \psi (at + r \cos \theta) d\theta ;$$

and since the first term vanishes this expression reduces itself to

$$\frac{a^2}{r} \int_0^\pi \psi' (at + r \cos \theta) \log (r \sin^2 \theta) \cos \theta d\theta$$

$$+ \frac{a^2}{r^2} \int_0^\pi \psi (at + r \cos \theta) d\theta,$$

and therefore to

$$\frac{a^2}{r} \cdot \frac{dz}{dr}.$$

Hence both these values of z satisfy the differential equation, which is therefore also satisfied by their sum, i.e. by the expression given in the question, and since this expression involves two arbitrary functions it is the general primitive of the differential equation.

WEDNESDAY, *Jan.* 18. 1½ *to* 4.

SENIOR EXAMINER.   Roman numbers.
JUNIOR EXAMINER.   Arabic numbers.

4. FIND the position of the point, the sum of the squares on the distances of which from the three sides of a triangle is the least possible; and prove that the angles, which the sides respectively subtend at this point, exceed the supplements of those which they subtend at the centre of gravity of the triangle by the respective angles of the triangle.

Let α, β, γ be the distances of the point required from the three sides of the triangle, a, b, c the lengths of those sides, K the area of the triangle. Then we have to make

$$r^2 = \alpha^2 + \beta^2 + \gamma^2, \text{ a maximum,}$$

α, β, γ being subject to the relation

$$a\alpha + b\beta + c\gamma = 2K.$$

Hence, by the method of indeterminate multipliers,

$$\frac{\alpha}{a} = \frac{\beta}{b} = \frac{\gamma}{c}.$$

The position of the point is thus determined. Now, fig. 41, let ABC be the triangle, P the required point, G the centre of gravity of the triangle. Then

$$\frac{\sin PAB}{\sin PAC} = \frac{\gamma}{\beta} = \frac{c}{b},$$

and
$$\frac{\sin GAB}{\sin GAC} = \frac{\text{area of triangle } GAB}{\text{area of triangle } GAC} \cdot \frac{GA.AC}{GA.AB} = \frac{AC}{AB} = \frac{b}{c},$$
whence,
$$\sin PAB : \sin PAC :: \sin GAC : \sin GAB,$$
and $\quad PAB + PAC = GAC + GAB;$
$$\therefore PAB = GAC, \ PAC = GAB;$$
similarly,
$$PBC = GBA, \ PBA = GBC, \ PCA = GCB, \ PCB = GCA.$$
Hence $\quad PCB = C - GCB,$
similarly, $\quad PBC = B - GBC;$
$$\therefore PCB + PBC = B + C - (GCB + GBC)$$
$$= B + C - \pi + BGC$$
$$= BGC - A;$$
$$\therefore \pi - BPC = BGC - A,$$
or $\quad BPC = \pi - BGC + A,$
similarly, $\quad CPA = \pi - CGA + B,$
$\quad APB = \pi - AGB + C.$

Hence the angles which the sides respectively subtend at P exceed the supplements of those which they respectively subtend at G, by A, B, C, respectively.

vi. Trace the curves represented by the equations
$$(x^2 - 4a^2) y^2 - 12a^2 x (a - y) = 0 \ldots\ldots\ldots (1),$$
$$\sin y - m \sin x = 0 \ldots\ldots\ldots (2).$$

In (1) explain the circumstance that the asymptotes parallel to the axis of y appear to contradict the statement of (v). In (2) distinguish between the cases in which $m > = $ or < 1.

First. The equation
$$(x^2 - 4a^2) y^2 - 12a^2 x (a - y) = 0$$
may be written in the form
$$(x^2 + 3ax - 4a^2) y^2 - 3ax (y - 2a)^2 = 0,$$
or $\quad\quad (x + 4a)(x - a) y^2 - 3ax (y - 2a)^2 = 0,$

when x is positive, it cannot be $< a$,

and when x is negative, ... $> 4a$.

When
	$x = 0,$	$y = 0,$
	$x = a,$	$y = 2a,$ two values,
	$x = 2a,$	$y = \infty$, or a,
	$x = \infty,$	$y^2 = 0,$
	$x = -2a,$	$y = \infty$, or a,
	$x = -4a,$	$y = 2a,$ two values,

near the origin $y^2 + 3ax = 0$.

The curve touches $x = a$, and $-4a$.

The axis of x and $x^2 - 4a^2 = 0$ are asymptotes.

The curve lies both above and below the axis of x at an infinite distance.

The form of the curve is as in fig. (42).

The asymptote $x = 2a$ is met in two points at an infinite distance by the branches to which it is itself an asymptote, and one more point where it meets the other parallel asymptote. Similarly for the asymptote $x = -2a$.

Secondly,
$$\sin y = m \sin x. \quad \text{Let } m < 1 \text{ and } = \sin \gamma.$$

For every value of x, if $y = \beta$, the equation will be satisfied by
$$2n\pi + \beta, \text{ and } (2n + 1) \pi - \beta,$$

$x = 0,$	$y = 0,$
x increases,	y increases,

$$x = \frac{\pi}{2}, \qquad y = \gamma,$$

x increases, $\qquad$ y diminishes,

$$x = \pi, \qquad y = 0,$$

and the shape is the same on the opposite side from $x = \pi$ to $x = 2\pi$, when it recurs, and similarly for x negative.

The shape is the same, see fig. 43, on the lines

$$y = 0, \quad y = \pm 2\pi, \quad y = \pm 4\pi, \ldots$$

and inverted on

$$y = \pm \pi, \quad y = \pm 3\pi, \ldots$$

If $m > 1$, the equation is the same interchanging x and y, and therefore the figure is the same, as if the above were turned through $90°$.

If $m = 1$, $y = 2n\pi + x$, or $(2n + 1)\pi - x$. See fig. 44.

10. One circle rolls within another; apply the above formula to find the area of the curve traced out by a given point within the rolling circle.

Let C be the centre of the fixed, O of the moving circle, P their point of contact at any time, fig. 45, V the point which traces out the required curve; let OV produced meet the circumference of the moving circle in Q, and let A be the point of the fixed circle with which Q originally coincided. Let $CP = a$, $OP = b$, $PCA = \theta$, so that $POQ = \frac{a}{b}\theta$, let $OV = c$, and let x, y be the co-ordinates of V. Then

$$x = (a - b)\cos\theta + c\cos\frac{a-b}{b}\theta,$$

$$y = (a - b)\sin\theta - c\sin\frac{a-b}{b}\theta;$$

$$\therefore xdy - ydx = (a-b)^2 d\theta - c^2\left(\frac{a-b}{b}\right)^2 d\theta$$

$$+ (a-b)c\cos\frac{a-2b}{b}\theta d\theta - \frac{(a-b)^2}{b}c\cos\frac{a-2b}{b}\theta d\theta,$$

and, integrating this between the limits 0 and 2π, we get for the area of the curve,

$$(a-b)^2\left(1-\frac{c^2}{b^2}\right)2\pi - \frac{a-b}{a-2b}bc\sin\frac{a-2b}{b}2\pi.$$

13. Define a developable surface; and, from your definition, deduce the partial differential equation of such surfaces.

Find the equation of the developable surface generated by the plane which moves in such a manner as to be always in contact with the surfaces

$$\frac{x^2}{a^2}+\frac{y^2}{b^2}+\frac{z^2}{c^2}=1,$$

$$\frac{x^2}{a^2-r^2}+\frac{y^2}{b^2-r^2}+\frac{z^2}{c^2-r^2}=1.$$

Let
$$lx+my+nz=1 \quad\ldots\ldots\ldots\ldots\ldots\ldots (1)$$
be the equation of a plane touching the ellipsoid
$$\frac{x^2}{a^2}+\frac{y^2}{b^2}+\frac{z^2}{c^2}=1.$$

We then have to find the locus of the ultimate intersections of (1), subject to the conditions

$$l^2a^2+m^2b^2+n^2c^2=1 \quad\ldots\ldots\ldots\ldots\ldots (2),$$
$$l^2\;\;+m^2\;\;+n^2\;\;=0 \quad\ldots\ldots\ldots\ldots\ldots (3).$$

[The equation (3) is impossible, but the form of the equation of the required surface may nevertheless be found. A similar method, moreover, may be applied to find the developable surface circumscribed about any two concentric and similarly situated surfaces of the second degree.]

Multiply (2) by λ, (3) by μ, and add to (1) and differentiate, and we get

$$x+\lambda la^2+\mu l=0 \quad\ldots\ldots\ldots\ldots\ldots\ldots (4),$$
$$y+\lambda mb^2+\mu m=0 \quad\ldots\ldots\ldots\ldots\ldots\ldots (5),$$
$$z+\lambda nc^2+\mu n=0 \quad\ldots\ldots\ldots\ldots\ldots\ldots (6),$$

(4) $l +$ (5) $m +$ (6) n gives
$$1 + \lambda = 0.$$
Hence $\quad x - la^2 + \mu l = 0,$

$$\therefore l = \frac{x}{a^2 - \mu}.$$

Similarly $\quad m = \dfrac{y}{b^2 - \mu}, \quad n = \dfrac{z}{c^2 - \mu}.$

Hence (1) becomes
$$\frac{x^2}{a^2 - \mu} + \frac{y^2}{b^2 - \mu} + \frac{z^2}{c^2 - \mu} = 1.$$

And (3) gives
$$\frac{x^2}{(a^2 - \mu)^2} + \frac{y^2}{(b^2 - \mu)^2} + \frac{z^2}{(c^2 - \mu)^2} = 0.$$

The latter of these equations is the differential of the former, hence the required result will be the same as that of eliminating μ between the equation

$$(\mu - a^2)(\mu - b^2)(\mu - c^2) + x^2(\mu - b^2)(\mu - c^2)$$
$$+ y^2(\mu - c^2)(\mu - a^2) + z^2(\mu - a^2)(\mu - b^2) = 0 \ldots\ldots (7),$$

and that obtained by differentiating it.

Now, writing (7) under the form
$$\mu^3 - P\mu^2 + Q\mu - R = 0,$$
its differential is
$$3\mu^2 - 2P\mu + Q = 0.$$

The result of the elimination of μ between these is
$$4(P^2 - 3Q)(Q^2 - 3PR) = (9R - PQ)^2.$$

The equation of the required surface is therefore given, by putting in the foregoing,

$P = a^2 + b^2 + c^2 - x^2 - y^2 - z^2,$
$Q = b^2c^2 + c^2a^2 + a^2b^2 - (b^2 + c^2)x^2 - (c^2 + a^2)y^2 - (a^2 + b^2)z^2,$
$R = a^2b^2c^2 - b^2c^2x^2 - c^2a^2y^2 - a^2b^2z^2.$

The required surface is, therefore, of the eighth degree.

14. Explain what is meant by $\Delta^n.0^m$; and prove that, if $f(e^t)$ be expanded in a series proceeding by ascending powers of t, the coefficient of t^m is $\dfrac{f(1+\Delta)\,0^m}{1.2\ldots\ldots m}$.

Prove that, if m be less than r,
$$\{1+\log(1+\Delta)\}^r.0^m = r(r-1)(r-2)\ldots(r-m+1).$$

By the theorem enunciated in the former part of the question,
$$\frac{\{1+\log(1+\Delta)\}^r.0^m}{1.2\ldots m}$$
will be the coefficient of t^m in $(1+\log e^t)^r$, that is, in $(1+t)^r$.

Hence
$$\frac{\{1+\log(1+\Delta)\}^r\,0^m}{1.2\ldots m} = \frac{r(r-1)\ldots(r-m+1)}{1.2\ldots m};$$
$$\therefore \{1+\log(1+\Delta)\}^r\,0^m = r(r-1)\ldots(r-m+1).$$

THURSDAY, *Jan.* 19. 9 *to* 12.

JUNIOR MODERATOR.

1. IF at the extremities P, Q of any two diameters CP, CQ of an ellipse, two tangents Pp, Qq be drawn cutting each other in T and the diameters produced in p and q, then the areas of the triangles TQp, TPq are equal.

Project the ellipse, orthogonally, into its auxiliary circle; then the areas of any two triangles TQp, TPq, fig. 46, in the primitive are in the ratio of their projections. But in the auxiliary circle these areas are equal by symmetry. Hence also they are equal in the primitive ellipse.

2. If a straight line CN be drawn from the centre to bisect that chord of the circle of curvature at any point P of an ellipse which is common to the ellipse and circle, and if it be produced to cut the ellipse in Q and the tangent in T, prove that $CP = CQ$, and that each is a mean proportional between CN and CT.

If two diameters be drawn in any ellipse, making equal angles with the major axis, then their conjugates will also make equal angles with the same axis. This is obvious from the consideration that the conjugate of any diameter is parallel to the tangents at the extremities of that diameter.

Now CP, fig. 47, by construction is the conjugate of the diameter parallel to PT, and CQ the conjugate of that parallel to PV. Also, by a known proposition in Conics, PT and PV

make equal angles with the major axis. Therefore CP, CQ make equal angles with the axis and are consequently equal.

Also by Goodwin's *Conics*, $CN . CT = CQ^2$.

3. If a, b, c be the sides of a triangle, and r the radius of the inscribed circle, then the distances of the radical centre of the three escribed circles from the sides of the triangle will be respectively

$$r\frac{b+c}{2a},\ r\frac{c+a}{2b},\ r\frac{a+b}{2c}.$$

Let ABC be the triangle, fig. 48, and let the side AB touch the two escribed circles in D and E. Now, by definition, the radical axis of the two circles bisects the common tangent DE, and is perpendicular to the straight line joining the centres of the circles. Also it is evident that the straight line joining the centres passes through C and bisects the angle exterior to ACB. Again, it is proved in most treatises on Trigonometry, that $DA = BE$, so that the middle points of DE and of the side AB are the same. Therefore the radical axis bisects the side AB and is parallel to the bisector of the angle ACB.

If $\alpha = 0$, $\beta = 0$, $\gamma = 0$ be the equations to the sides of the triangle, the equation to any straight line parallel to the bisector of the angle C is

$$\alpha - \beta = \text{constant},$$

but since this passes through the middle point of AB, it must be satisfied by $\alpha = \frac{c}{2}\sin B,\ \beta = \frac{c}{2}\sin \alpha$.

Hence the equation to the radical axis is

$$\alpha - \beta = \frac{c}{2}(\sin B - \sin A).$$

Similarly, another radical axis will be

$$\beta - \gamma = \frac{c}{2}(\sin C - \sin B).$$

But
$$a\alpha + b\beta + c\gamma = 2\Delta,$$
where Δ is the area of the triangle. Solving these equations to determine β, remembering that
$$\Delta = \frac{ac \sin B}{2},$$
we get
$$\beta = r\frac{c+a}{2b},$$
and the values of γ and α may be written down from symmetry.

Cor. If the radical centre coincides with the centre of the inscribed circle, the triangle must be equilateral.

4. Two equal heavy particles are connected by a string which passes through a small smooth ring. Prove that the equation to the plane vertical curve on which the particles will rest in all positions is
$$r \cos \theta = a + \psi(r) - \psi(l-r),$$
where θ is the angle the radius vector makes with the vertical, l is the length of the string, ψ an arbitrary function, and a an arbitrary constant.

Take the smooth fixed ring as origin, and the axis of x vertical. Let x, r, x', r' be the co-ordinates of the two particles. Then by virtual velocities we have
$$dx + dx' = 0;$$
$$\therefore x + x' = c,$$
also
$$r + r' = l.$$

Let $x = \phi(r)$ be the equation to the curve, then $x' = \phi(r')$, and we have the functional equation
$$\phi(r) + \phi(l-r) = c.$$

Solving this in the manner exhibited in Herschel's examples, we get
$$\phi(r) = a + \psi(r) + \psi(l-r).$$

5. If four equal particles, attracting each other with forces which vary as the distance, slide along the arc of a smooth ellipse, they cannot generally be in equilibrium unless placed at the extremities of the axes; but if a fifth equal particle be fixed at any point and attract the other four according to the same law, there will be equilibrium if the distances of the four particles from the semi-axis major be the roots of the equation

$$(y^2 - b^2)\left(y + \frac{b^2 q}{5a^2 - 3b^2}\right)^2 = -\frac{a^2 b^2 p^2}{(3a^2 - 5b^2)^2} y^2,$$

where p and q are the distances of the fifth particle from the axis minor and axis major respectively.

If the four particles be placed on an arc of an ellipse in equilibrium, the resultant attraction on any particle must be normal to the curve. Hence, by Todhunter's *Statics*, Art. 220, the four normals at the four particles must meet in their centre of gravity.

Let x, y be the co-ordinates of any particle, then the equation to the normal is

$$y' - y = \frac{a^2 y}{b^2 x}(x' - x) \quad \ldots\ldots\ldots\ldots (1).$$

Let hk be the co-ordinates of the point in which the four normals meet, then

$$k - y = \frac{a^2 y}{b^2 x}(h - x) \quad \ldots\ldots\ldots\ldots (2),$$

also

$$\left[\frac{x}{a}\right]^2 + \left[\frac{y}{b}\right]^2 = 1 \quad \ldots\ldots\ldots\ldots (3).$$

Eliminating x we get

$$(a^2 - b^2)^2 y^4 + 2b^2 k (a^2 - b^2) y^3 + \{b^4 k^2 + a^2 h^2 - (a^2 - b^2)^2\} b^2 y^2$$
$$- 2b^4 k (a^2 - b^2) y - b^6 k^2 = 0 \quad \ldots\ldots\ldots\ldots (4),$$

Since k is the ordinate of the centre of gravity, k is one-fourth of the sum of the roots of this equation;

$$\therefore\ 4k = -\frac{2b^2 k (a^2 - b^2)}{(a^2 - b^2)^2} \quad \ldots\ldots\ldots\ldots (5).$$

This equation can only be satisfied by
$$a^2 - b^2 = 0, \quad \text{or} \quad a^2 + 7b^2 = 0,$$
or by $k = 0$. Taking the latter supposition, the equation (4) reduces to
$$\left.\begin{array}{r} y = 0, \\ (a^2 - b^2)^2 y^2 + b^2 \{a^2 h - (a^2 - b^2)^2\} = 0 ; \end{array}\right\}$$
hence two of the particles must be situated at the extremities of the major axis. To find the positions of the other two, write for y^2, its value obtained from (3), and we get
$$h^2 = e^2 x^2,$$
but since h is the abscissa of the centre of gravity, we have $h = \dfrac{x}{2}$: hence this equation can only be satisfied, *first* by $x = 0$, and then the four particles are at the extremities of the two axes: *secondly* by $e = \dfrac{1}{\sqrt{2}}$, and in this particular ellipse there will be equilibrium if two of the particles are at the extremities of the major axis, and the other two are at the extremities of *any* ordinate.

The case $a^2 + 7b^2 = 0$ is impossible. In the case $a^2 = b^2$, the ellipse becomes a circle, and equation (4) reduces to
$$y^2 = \frac{b^4}{b^2 + a^2 \left(\dfrac{h}{k}\right)^2}.$$

But since h and k in this case must both vanish because all the normals pass through the centre, this expression may have any value. Hence there will be equilibrium in a circle if the four particles are at the extremities of any two diameters.

If we have *five* particles, it is necessary that the point (hk) should coincide with the centre of gravity of the five masses. Hence equation (4) becomes

and similarly
$$5k = -\frac{2b^2k}{a^2-b^2}+q,$$
$$5h = \frac{2a^2h}{a^2-b^2}+p,$$

substituting these in equations (2) and (3) we get

$$\left(y+\frac{b^2q}{5a^2-3b^2}\right)^2(y^2-b^2) = -\frac{a^2b^4p^2}{(3a^2-5b^2)^2}\cdot y^2,$$

the required result.

6. A heavy string is placed in equilibrium on a smooth sphere; prove that, if θ be the length of the spherical arc drawn from the highest point of the sphere perpendicular to the great circle touching the string at any point P, then

$$\sin\theta = \frac{a}{z+b},$$

where z is the perpendicular from P on any horizontal plane, and a, b are constants.

Shew that the form of the string can be a circle only when its plane is vertical or horizontal.

Let z be the highest point of the sphere, fig. 49, AB the string, and PQN the great circle touching it along the element PQ.

Let T be the tension at P, then resolving the forces on the element PQ along its arc, we get

$$dT = gdz;$$
$$\therefore T = gz + c.$$

Again, take moments about the vertical through z. Resolving T perpendicular to the axis, we get $T\sin zPN$, and the moment is therefore

$$T\sin zPN \cdot \sin zP = T\sin\theta,$$

hence $$d(T\sin\theta) = 0;$$

$$\therefore T \sin \theta = c';$$

$$\therefore \sin \theta = \frac{a}{z+b},$$

where a and b are arbitrary.

The curve of the string could not be a circle, for the altitude of the centre of gravity must be a maximum or minimum. Now unless the plane of the circle be vertical or horizontal, a slight motion, without change of form, will clearly elevate or depress the centre.

7. If three particles of masses m, m', m'' attracting each other start from rest, shew that if at any instant parallels to their directions of motion be drawn so as to form a triangle the momenta of the several particles are as the sides of that triangle.

Let v, v', v'' be the velocities of the particles. Since the three particles start from rest, the area conserved round any point is zero. Now the area conserved by any particle of mass m moving with velocity v is mvp, where p is the length of the perpendicular from the origin on the direction of motion. Hence

$$mv \cdot p + m'v' \cdot p' + m''v'' \cdot p'' = 0.$$

Therefore if three forces represented by mv, $m'v'$, $m''v''$ were to act along the directions of motion, the sum of their moments about every point would be zero. Therefore these forces are in equilibrium, and if a triangle be constructed by drawing lines parallel to their directions, the forces will be proportional to the sides of that triangle.

Hence also the three directions of motion being produced meet always in one point O.

Let F, F', F'' be the resultant forces on the three particles each due to the attraction of the other two. Then, these being the resultants, two and two, of all the internal forces of the system, must balance each other. Therefore the three forces F, F', F'' meet in a point O', and are proportional to the sides of a triangle formed by drawing parallels to the straight lines joining O' to the particles.

The points O, O' are not in general the same, nor are they fixed in space. If the law of attraction be directly as the distance, they both coincide with the centre of gravity of the system.

8. If from any point on a surface a number of geodesic lines be drawn in all directions, shew (1) that those which have the greatest and least curvature of torsion bisect the angles between the principal sections, and (2) that the radius of torsion of any line, making an angle θ with a principal section, is given by the equation

$$\frac{1}{R} = \left(\frac{1}{\rho_1} - \frac{1}{\rho_2}\right)\sin\theta\cos\theta,$$

where ρ_1, ρ_2 are the radii of curvature of the principal sections.

Take the given point as origin O, and the normal as the axis of z, and let the equation to the surface be

$$2z = \phi(x, y)$$
$$= ax^2 + by^2 + \ldots$$

Let OP be any geodesic line and ON the projection of OP on the plane of xy.

The osculating plane of any geodesic line contains the normal to the surface on which it is drawn. Hence NOZ is the osculating plane at O, and also the osculating plane at P contains the normal to the surface at P.

Let $d\epsilon$ be the angle between two consecutive normal planes to the curve, du the angle between two consecutive osculating planes. Then clearly the normal OZ is turned into the consecutive normal to the surface at P, by turning it, first through the angle $d\epsilon$, then through du; and the planes of these angles are at right angles.

The equation to the normal at P is

$$\frac{\xi - x}{ax} = \frac{\eta - y}{by} = \frac{\zeta - z}{-1};$$

$$\therefore \cos du . \cos d\epsilon = \frac{-1}{\sqrt{(1 + a^2x^2 + b^2y^2)}};$$

$$\therefore \overline{d\theta}|^2 + \overline{d\epsilon}|^2 = a^2 x^2 + b^2 y^2;$$

$$\therefore \frac{1}{R^2} + \frac{1}{\rho^2} = a^2 \cos^2\theta + b^2 \sin^2\theta.$$

But by Euler's theorem since $a = \dfrac{1}{\rho_1}$, $b = \dfrac{1}{\rho_2}$,

$$\frac{1}{\rho} = a\cos^2\theta + b\sin^2\theta;$$

therefore substituting, we get

$$\frac{1}{R} = (a-b)\sin\theta\cos\theta$$

$$= \left(\frac{1}{\rho_1} - \frac{1}{\rho_2}\right)\sin\theta\cos\theta.$$

This is a maximum or minimum when $\theta = \dfrac{\pi}{4}$, hence the tangents, the geodesic lines of greatest and least torsion, bisect the angles between the principal sections.

If R_0 be the least radius of torsion, and R the radius of a geodesic line making an angle ϕ with it, then the above expression becomes

$$R = \frac{R_0}{\cos 2\phi}.$$

The expression for R may also be put into the form

$$\frac{1}{R} = -\frac{1}{2}\frac{d}{d\theta}\left(\frac{1}{\rho}\right).$$

9. If du and $d\epsilon$ be the angles of torsion and contingence of any curve of double curvature, and if $\sin\phi$ be the ratio of the radius of circular curvature to the radius of spherical curvature, prove that the square of the angle of contingence of the locus of the centres of circular curvature is

$$\overline{d\phi + du}|^2 + \cos^2\phi \,\overline{d\epsilon}|^2.$$

Let CC', fig. 50, be an element of the locus of the centres of circular curvature corresponding to a point A on the original curve. This element ultimately lies in the normal plane at A, let it make an angle ϕ with the principal normal AC produced. Now any element CC' is brought into the position of the next by turning it, first, through an angle du round the tangent AA' to the curve, secondly, through an angle $d\epsilon$ round a perpendicular CO at C to the osculating plane CAA'; the element has thus been brought into the consecutive normal plane to the original curve, and we have therefore, thirdly, only to increase ϕ by 2ϕ.

The change may therefore be effected by turning CC' in two planes at right angles to each other through the two angles $C'CP = du + d\phi$, and $PCQ = d\epsilon \cos \phi$.

Therefore if $d\psi$ be the angle between the old and new positions of CC',

$$\cos d\psi = \cos (du + d\phi) \cdot \cos (d\epsilon \cos \phi),$$

or $\overline{d\psi}|^2 = (du + d\phi)^2 + \overline{d\epsilon}|^2 \cos^2 \phi.$

10. A particle is projected with velocity V along an infinitely thin ellipsoidal shell attracting according to the law of nature; prove that when it leaves the ellipsoid the perpendicular from the centre on the tangent plane is

$$\sqrt[3]{\left(\frac{4\pi\mu R^2 P^2}{V^2}\right)},$$

where R is the radius-vector parallel to the initial direction of motion, and P the perpendicular on the tangent, μ the attraction of a mass equivalent to a unit of area of the ellipsoid at a unit of distance.

First we must find the attraction of the ellipsoidal shell on the particle. Let P be the position of the particle at any instant, take a point Q just inside the shell, and situated on the normal at P. Round P take any very small area A which may be ultimately considered as plane. Since the point P is on the ellipsoid, its distance is infinitely small compared with the linear dimensions of the area A. Hence the attraction of A on P or Q is ultimately the same as that of an infinite plane on a point at a finite distance from it, and is therefore normal and equal to $2\pi\mu$. The attraction of the whole ellipsoidal shell on Q is zero, hence the attraction on Q of the whole shell except the area A is $2\pi\mu$. But it is evident that the whole shell less the area A exerts equal attractions on P and Q, because the distance PQ diminishes without limit compared with the distance of P from the nearest point of the attractive mass. Therefore the attraction of the whole shell on P is normal and equal to $4\pi\mu$.

Now since this attraction is normal to the path of the particle, its velocity will be always the same and equal to V; and it will describe a geodesic line on the ellipsoid.

The pressure on the ellipsoid will be $4\pi\mu - \dfrac{V^2}{\rho}$, where ρ is the radius of curvature. Hence when the particle leaves the ellipsoid, we have

$$4\pi\mu = \frac{V^2}{\rho}.$$

Now, because the path is a geodesic line, $\rho = \dfrac{r^3}{c^2}$, where r is the radius vector of the ellipsoid parallel to the direction of motion, and c^2 is a constant $= PR$. (See Hymers' *Solid Geometry*, Problems on Sect. x). Hence we have

$$r = \sqrt[3]{\left(\frac{V^2 . PR}{4\pi\mu}\right)}.$$

If p be the perpendicular from the centre on the tangent plane at the point where the particle leaves the ellipsoid, we also have

$$p = \sqrt[3]{\left(\frac{4\pi\mu . R^2 . P^2}{V^2}\right)}.$$

Now the shell has been supposed bounded by similar ellipsoids, hence μ is really variable and proportional to the thickness h of the shell. Let $\mu = \mu_0 h$. Also by similar figures this thickness is proportional to p; let n be the infinitely small ratio of the thickness of the shell at the extremity of any axis to that semi-axis. Then $h = np$; therefore $\mu = \mu_0 n . p$, and let $m = \mu_0 n$. Then substituting in the above expression, we get

$$p = \sqrt{\left(\frac{4\pi m R^2 P^2}{V^2}\right)}.$$

11. An infinitely thin ellipsoidal shell attracting according to the law of nature is bounded by two similar and similarly situated ellipsoids. A very small piece is cut out of the shell and replaced in its original position. Shew that the force necessary to hold the piece in equilibrium is proportional to the square of the thickness of the shell.

Let dB be any element of the small piece of area B cut out of the ellipsoid. Round dB describe a small area A which may be ultimately considered plane and with respect to which dB is infinitely small. Then the attraction of A on this element dB of itself is clearly zero. Let f be the attraction of the remainder of the shell on a unit of mass supposed collected at dB. Then, since the shell is infinitely thin, we may consider f to be the same throughout the thickness h of dB, and therefore the force necessary to hold dB in equilibrium is $f . dB . h$. But we have proved that $f = 2\pi\mu . h$, hence the force $= 2\pi\mu dB . h^2$. Hence the force on the whole very small area B is $2\pi\mu B . h^2$.

12. A sphere of radius a is suspended from a fixed point by a string of length l and is made to rotate about a vertical axis with an angular velocity ω. Prove that, if the string make small oscillations about its mean position, the motion of the centre of gravity will be represented by a series of terms of the form

$$L \cos (\kappa t + M),$$

where the several values of κ are the roots of the equation

$$(l\kappa^2 - g)\left(\kappa^2 - \omega\kappa - \frac{5g}{2a}\right) = \frac{5}{2}g\kappa^2.$$

Let G be the centre of gravity of the sphere, BGC the diameter to the extremity of which the string is tied. Take the fixed extremity of the string as the origin, and fixed axes in space, so that g acts parallel to the positive direction of the axis of z. Let $\omega_1, \omega_2, \omega_3$ be the angular velocities of the sphere about diameters parallel to the axes. Let P, Q be the direction-cosines of GC and $P'Q'$ of the string referred to the axes x and y.

The squares of small quantities being neglected according to the usual rule, it is also obvious that the tension of the string will be the weight of the sphere.

The equations of motion are therefore

$$\frac{d\omega_1}{dt} + n\omega_2 = \frac{\text{moment of forces}}{A}$$

$$\left. \begin{array}{l} = \dfrac{ag}{A}(Q-Q'), \\[2mm] \dfrac{d\omega_2}{dt} - n\omega_1 = \dfrac{ag}{A}(P'-P), \end{array} \right\}$$

where A is the square of the radius of gyration of the sphere about a diameter $= \dfrac{2}{5}a^2$.

Also $\omega_2 =$ rate at which GC approaches

$$x = -\frac{d}{dt}(\cos^{-1}P) = \frac{dP}{dt}.$$

Similarly

$$\omega_1 = -\frac{dQ}{dt}.$$

If xy be the co-ordinates of the centre of gravity, we have

$$\left. \begin{array}{l} \dfrac{d^2x}{dt^2} = -gP, \\[2mm] \dfrac{d^2y}{dt^2} = -gQ. \end{array} \right\}$$

Also $\qquad x = lP' + aP, \quad y = lQ' + aQ.$

Substituting for x, y, ω_1, ω_2 their values in terms of P, Q, P', Q', we get

$$\frac{d^2Q}{dt^2} - n\frac{dP}{dt} = \frac{ag}{A}(Q'-Q),$$
$$\frac{d^2P}{dt^2} + n\frac{dQ}{dt} = \frac{ag}{A}(P'-P),$$
$$l\frac{d^2P'}{dt^2} + a\frac{d^2P}{dt^2} = -gP',$$
$$l\frac{d^2Q'}{dt^2} + a\frac{d^2Q}{dt^2} = -gQ'.$$

To solve these put $P = L\cos(\kappa t + M)$, $Q = M\sin(\kappa t + M)$, $P' = L'\cos(\kappa t + M)$, $Q' = M'\sin(\kappa t + M)$, we get

$$L'(g - l\kappa^2) = a\kappa^2 L,$$
$$M'(g - l\kappa^2) = a\kappa^2 M,$$
$$L\left(\frac{ag}{A} - \kappa^2\right) - \frac{ag}{A}L' = -nM\kappa,$$
$$M\left(\frac{ag}{A} - \kappa^2\right) - \frac{ag}{A}M' = -nL\kappa.$$

Eliminating the ratios of L, M, L', M', we get

$$(l\kappa^2 - g)\left(\kappa^2 - n\kappa - \frac{ag}{A}\right) = \frac{a^2 g}{A}\kappa^2;$$

when we put $A = \frac{2}{5}a^2$, this reduces to the result given in the question.

13. A string is in equilibrium in the form of a circle about a centre of force in the centre. If the string be now cut at any point A, prove that the tension at any point P is instantaneously changed in the ratio of $1 - \dfrac{\epsilon^{\pi-\theta} + \epsilon^{-(\pi-\theta)}}{\epsilon^\pi + \epsilon^{-\pi}} : 1$, where θ is the angle subtended at the centre by the arc AP.

This is a particular case of a more general proposition. Suppose a string to be in equilibrium in any curve in one plane under the action of any forces. Let Pds, Qds be the resolved parts of these along the tangent and normal to any element ds. In order to refer the motion to moving axes, let u, v be the velocities of the element along the tangent and normal. Then the equations are

$$\frac{du}{dt} - v\frac{d\phi}{dt} = P + \frac{dT}{ds} \quad \ldots \ldots \ldots \ldots (1),$$

$$\frac{dv}{dt} + u\frac{d\phi}{dt} = Q + \frac{T}{\rho} \quad \ldots \ldots \ldots \ldots (2),$$

where T is the tension, ρ the radius of curvature, and ϕ the angle the tangent makes with any fixed straight line.

In the beginning of the motion just after the string is cut, we may reject the squares of small quantities, hence $v\frac{d\phi}{dt}$ and $u\frac{d\phi}{dt}$ may be neglected.

The geometrical equations are to be found from the condition that any element $PQ = ds$ of the string is inextensible. The tangential and normal velocities of P and Q are respectively u, v and $u + du$, $v + dv$. Hence the velocity of separation of P and Q along the tangent is $du - vd\phi$, which must be zero, and the velocity of rotation of Q round P is $dv + ud\phi$, which must be $ds \cdot \frac{d\phi}{dt}$. Hence we have the two equations

$$\frac{du}{ds} - \frac{v}{\rho} = 0 \quad \ldots \ldots \ldots \ldots (3),$$

$$\frac{dv}{ds} + \frac{u}{\rho} = \frac{d\phi}{dt} \quad \ldots \ldots \ldots \ldots (4).$$

Differentiating (3) we get

$$\frac{d^2u}{ds\,dt} = \frac{1}{\rho}\frac{dv}{dt},$$

since the small term $v\frac{d\left(\frac{1}{\rho}\right)}{dt}$ may be neglected in the beginning of the motion.

Substituting from equations (1) and (2)

$$\frac{dP}{ds} + \frac{d^2T}{ds^2} = \frac{Q}{\rho} + \frac{T}{\rho^2};$$

$$\therefore \frac{d^2T}{ds^2} - \frac{T}{\rho^2} = -\frac{dP}{ds} + \frac{Q}{\rho}.$$

This is the general equation to determine the tension of the string at the instant after the string is cut.

If the string be in the form of a circle, as in the question, $Q = -F$ is independent of s and $B = 0$, and $\rho = a$ the radius;

$$\therefore \frac{d^2T}{ds^2} - \frac{T}{a^2} = \frac{-F}{a}.$$

Now $s = a\theta$, hence we get

$$T = Fa + A\epsilon^\theta + B\epsilon^{-\theta}.$$

To determine the arbitrary constants we observe that $T = 0$ when $\theta = 0$, and $\theta = 2\pi$;

$$\therefore T = Fa \left\{ 1 - \frac{\epsilon^{(\pi-\theta)} + \epsilon^{-(\pi-\theta)}}{\epsilon^\pi + \epsilon^{-\pi}} \right\}.$$

But just before the string was cut we have

$$T = Fa.$$

Hence the result given in the question follows at once.

If the string be a catenary under the action of gravity, we have

$$P = -g\frac{s}{\sqrt{(s^2+c^2)}} \quad \text{and} \quad Q = -\frac{gc}{\sqrt{(s^2+c^2)}},$$

whence
$$\frac{dP}{ds^2} = \frac{Q}{\rho}.$$

The equation becomes

$$\frac{d^2T}{ds^2} - \frac{T}{\rho^2} = 0,$$

which has been integrated in a previous question.

If the string be in the form of an equiangular spiral under the action of a central repulsive force in the pole varying inversely as the cube of the distance, the resulting equation can be easily integrated.

14. An inelastic string is suspended from two fixed points so that it hangs in the form of a catenary of which the parameter is c. Suppose it to make small oscillations in a vertical plane, prove the equation

$$\frac{d^2\phi}{dt^2} = \frac{g}{c}\cos^3\alpha\left\{\frac{d^2\phi}{d\alpha^2} + 4\phi + f(t)\right\},$$

where α is the angle the tangent at any point makes with the horizon when the string is at rest, and $\alpha + \phi$ is the value of the same angle at the time t.

Shew that there are sufficient data to determine all the arbitrary functions.

Let u, v be the velocities of any element ds of the string resolved along the tangent and normal. Then the general equations of motion of the string are

$$\left.\begin{array}{c}\dfrac{du}{dt} - v\dfrac{d\phi}{dt} = -g\sin(\alpha+\phi) + \dfrac{dT'}{ds}, \\[2mm] \dfrac{dv}{dt} + u\dfrac{d\phi}{dt} = -g\cos(\alpha+\phi) + \dfrac{T'd\phi}{ds}, \end{array}\right\}$$

where T' is the tension. Now the tension when the string is at rest is $gy = \dfrac{gc}{\cos\alpha}$. Let $T' = \dfrac{gc}{\cos\alpha} + T$. Substitute and remember that in small oscillations we may neglect the squares of the small quantities u, v, ϕ, we get

$$\frac{du}{dt} = -g\cos\alpha \cdot \phi + \frac{\cos^2\alpha}{c}\frac{dT}{d\alpha}\dots\dots\dots\dots\dots(1),$$

$$\frac{dv}{dt} = g\sin\alpha \cdot \phi + g\cos\alpha \cdot \frac{d\phi}{d\alpha} + \frac{\cos^2\alpha}{c}T\dots\dots(2).$$

We have also the two general geometrical equations

$$\begin{aligned}\frac{du}{ds}-\frac{v}{\rho}&=0,\\ \frac{dv}{ds}+\frac{u}{\rho}&=\frac{d\phi}{dt},\end{aligned}\Bigg\}$$

where $\dfrac{1}{\rho}=\dfrac{d\alpha}{ds}+\dfrac{d\phi}{ds}$ is the reciprocal of the radius of curvature. Changing the independent variable and neglecting the squares of small quantities these reduce to

$$\frac{d^2u}{d\alpha^2}+u=\frac{c}{\cos^3\alpha}\frac{d\phi}{dt}\quad\ldots\ldots\ldots\ldots\ldots(3).$$

For the sake of brevity put $u'v'\phi''$ for $\dfrac{du}{dt}$, $\dfrac{dv}{dt}$, $\dfrac{d^2\phi}{dt^2}$ respectively.

In order to eliminate T from equations (1) and (2) differentiate the second, we get

$$\frac{d^2u'}{d\alpha^2}=g\cos\alpha\,\phi+g\cos\alpha\,\frac{d^2\phi}{d\alpha^2}+\frac{\cos^2\alpha}{c}\frac{dT}{d\alpha}-\frac{2\cos\alpha\sin\alpha}{c}T;$$

$$\therefore\ \frac{d^2u'}{d\alpha^2}-u'=g\cos\alpha\left(\frac{d^2\phi}{d\alpha^2}+2\phi\right)-\frac{2\cos\alpha\sin\alpha}{c}T.$$

Eliminating T from this by means of (2), we get

$$\cos\alpha\left(\frac{d^2u'}{d\alpha^2}+u'\right)+2\left(\sin\alpha\,\frac{du'}{d\alpha}-u'\cos\alpha\right)=g\cos^3\alpha\,\frac{d^2\phi}{d\alpha^2}$$
$$+2g\sin\alpha\cos\alpha\,\frac{d\phi}{d\alpha}+2g\phi\ \ldots\ldots\ldots(4).$$

But by (3)

$$\frac{d^2u'}{d\alpha^2}+u'=\frac{c}{\cos^3\alpha}\phi''';$$

$$\therefore\ \sin\alpha\,\frac{du'}{d\alpha}-u'\cos\alpha=c\int\frac{\sin\alpha}{\cos^3\alpha}\phi''',$$

substitute these in (4), we get

$$\frac{c}{\cos\alpha}\phi'' + 2c\int\frac{\sin\alpha}{\cos^2\alpha}\phi'' = g\left(\cos^2\alpha\frac{d^2\phi}{d\alpha^2} + 2\sin\alpha\cos\alpha\frac{d\phi}{d\alpha} + 2\phi\right).$$

Differentiate again, we have

$$\frac{c}{\cos\alpha}\frac{d\phi''}{d\alpha} + \frac{3c\sin\alpha}{\cos^2\alpha}\phi'' = g\cos^2\alpha\left(\frac{d^3\phi}{d\alpha^3} + 4\frac{d\phi}{d\alpha}\right);$$

$$\therefore \frac{\cos^3\alpha\dfrac{d\phi''}{d\alpha} + 3\cos^2\alpha\sin\alpha\phi''}{\cos^6\alpha} = \frac{g}{c}\left(\frac{d^3\phi}{d\alpha^3} + 4\frac{d\phi}{d\alpha}\right);$$

integrating both sides, we have

$$\frac{\phi''}{\cos^3\alpha} = \frac{g}{c}\left\{\frac{d^2\phi}{d\alpha^2} + 4\phi + f^{(t)}\right\},$$

which is the same as the result given in the question.

An expression for the tension may be found as follows. Differentiating (2) and adding the result to (1), we obviously get

$$\frac{c}{\cos^2\alpha}\frac{d^2\phi}{dt^2} = g\cos\alpha\frac{d^2\phi}{d\alpha^2} + 2\frac{\cos^2\alpha}{c}\frac{dT}{d\alpha} + \frac{T}{c}\frac{d\cos^2\alpha}{d\alpha},$$

or $\cos\alpha\dfrac{dT}{d\alpha} - \sin\alpha \cdot T = \dfrac{c^2}{2}\left(\dfrac{1}{\cos^3\alpha}\dfrac{d^2\phi}{dt^2} - \dfrac{g}{c}\dfrac{d^2\phi}{d\alpha^2}\right)$

$$= \frac{c^2}{2}\{4\phi + f^{(t)}\};$$

$$\therefore \cos\alpha \cdot T = \frac{c^2}{2}\int\{4\phi + f^{(t)}\}\,d\alpha;$$

$$\therefore T = \frac{c^2 f^{(t)}}{2}\cdot\frac{\alpha}{\cos\alpha}2c^2\int\phi\,d\alpha.$$

THURSDAY, *Jan.* 19. 1½ *to* 4.

SENIOR MODERATOR. Roman numbers.
JUNIOR MODERATOR. Arabic numbers.

1. FIND a superior limit to the numerical values of x consistent with the convergency of the series

$$x + \frac{2^2 x^2}{1.2} + \frac{3^3 x^3}{1.2.3} + \ldots + \frac{n^n . x^n}{1.2\ldots n} + \ldots$$

Here
$$u_{n+1} = \frac{(n+1)^{n+1} . x^{n+1}}{\lfloor n+1},$$

$$u_n = \frac{n^n . x^n}{\lfloor n};$$

$$\therefore \frac{u_{n+1}}{u_n} = \frac{(n+1)^{n+1}}{n^n} \cdot \frac{x}{n+1} = \left(\frac{n+1}{n}\right)^n x = \left(1 + \frac{1}{n}\right)^n x;$$

$$\therefore lt_{n=\infty} \frac{u_{n+1}}{u_n} = lt_{n=\infty} \left(1 + \frac{1}{n}\right)^n x = ex,$$

and the superior limit to the values of x is therefore $\frac{1}{e}$.

2. If the sides of a spherical triangle be small compared with the radius of the sphere, then each angle of the spherical triangle exceeds by one-third of the spherical excess the corresponding angle of the plane triangle, the sides of which are of the same length as the sides of the spherical triangle.

If the sides of a right-angled plane triangle of given area be bent so as to form a spherical triangle on a given sphere of great radius, the alteration of area in the triangle is very nearly proportional to the square of the hypothenuse.

It is proved in Todhunter's *Spherical Trigonometry*, Art. 109, that the area of any spherical triangle whose sides are $\alpha\beta\gamma$ exceeds that of the plane triangle by the fraction $\dfrac{\alpha^2+\beta^2+\gamma^2}{24r^2}$ of the latter, where r is the radius of the sphere. If the plane triangle be right-angled $\alpha^2+\beta^2=\gamma^2$, and it may be proved in exactly the same way, that the alteration in area is $=\dfrac{\gamma^2}{2r^2}$ of the plane triangle. This expression varies as γ^2, because by the question the area of the plane triangle is constant.

3. Two tangents OA, OB are drawn to a conic, and are cut in P and Q by a variable tangent; prove that the locus of the centres of all circles described about the triangle OPQ is an hyperbola.

Taking OA, OB as axes, let the equation to the tangent PQ be

$$\frac{x}{a}+\frac{y}{\beta}-1=0 \quad\ldots\ldots\ldots\ldots\ldots (1),$$

and the equation to the conic

$$xy = \kappa \left(\frac{x}{a}+\frac{y}{b}-1\right)^2 \quad\ldots\ldots\ldots\ldots (2).$$

Then the equation to the circle is

$$x^2+y^2+2xy\cos\omega = ax+\beta y \quad\ldots\ldots\ldots\ldots (3).$$

Then since (1) touches (2) the roots of the equation

$$\sqrt{\left(\frac{xy}{\kappa}\right)} = x\left(\frac{1}{a}-\frac{1}{a}\right)+y\left(\frac{1}{b}-\frac{1}{\beta}\right)$$

must be equal;

$$\therefore \left(\frac{1}{a}-\frac{1}{a}\right)\left(\frac{1}{\beta}-\frac{1}{b}\right) = \frac{1}{4\kappa} \quad\ldots\ldots\ldots\ldots (4).$$

To determine the centre of (3), we have

$$\left.\begin{array}{l} x+y\cos\omega = \dfrac{a}{2}, \\[4pt] y+x\cos\omega = \dfrac{\beta}{2}. \end{array}\right\}$$

Substituting in (4) the equation to the required locus is

$$(x + y \cos \omega)(y + x \cos \omega)$$
$$= \frac{2b(x + y \cos \omega) + 2a(y + x \cos \omega) - ab}{4 - \dfrac{ab}{\kappa}},$$

which is evidently an hyperbola.

If the given conic be a parabola, we must have $4\kappa = ab$, hence we get for the locus

$$\frac{x + y \cos \omega}{a} + \frac{y + x \cos \omega}{b} = \tfrac{1}{2},$$

which is a straight line. This is evident, *a priori*, for it is a known property that all these circles pass through the focus.

iv. If u be a function of three independent variables x, y, z, which are connected by three equations with three new independent variables ξ, η, ζ, shew how to express the partial differential coefficients of u, to the first and second orders respectively, with respect to x, y, z, in terms of the corresponding partial differential coefficients with respect to ξ, η, ζ.

Apply this method to prove that, if at a certain point in a surface $r = t$ and $s = 0$ when the axes of x and y are taken parallel to a particular pair of lines, at right angles to each other, in the tangent plane at that point, the axis of z being normal, then the following relations will hold at that point whatever be the direction of the co-ordinate axes provided they be rectangular, viz.

$$\frac{r}{1 + p^2} = \frac{s}{pq} = \frac{t}{1 + q^2};$$

where p, q, r, s, t, denote

$$\frac{dz}{dx}, \ \frac{dz}{dy}, \ \frac{d^2z}{dx^2}, \ \frac{d^2z}{dx\,dy}, \ \frac{d^2z}{dy^2},$$

respectively.

Let the equation to the surface referred to the original axes, whereof that of z is normal and those of x and y are at right angles to each and tangential, be

$$u = z - f(x, y) = 0,$$

let ξ, η, ζ be the new axes, and let the relations between the old and new variables be

$$x = a_1\xi + b_1\eta + c_1\zeta,$$
$$y = a_2\xi + b_2\eta + c_2\zeta,$$
$$z = a_3\xi + b_3\eta + c_3\zeta;$$

$$\therefore \frac{du}{d\xi} = a_1\frac{du}{dx} + a_2\frac{du}{dy} + a_3\frac{du}{dz} = -a_1\frac{dz}{dx} - a_2\frac{dz}{dy} + a_3 = a_3;$$

$$\because \frac{dz}{dx} = 0 \ \frac{dz}{dy} = 0.$$

Similarly for $\dfrac{du}{d\eta}$ and $\dfrac{du}{d\zeta}$;

again,

$$\frac{d^2u}{d\xi^2} = -a_1^2\frac{d^2z}{dx^2} - 2a_1a_2\frac{d^2z}{dx\,dy} - a_2^2\frac{d^2z}{dy^2} = -(1-a_3^2)\,r;$$

$$\because \frac{d^2z}{dx^2} = \frac{d^2z}{dy^2} = r, \text{ and } \frac{d^2z}{dx\,dy} = 0.$$

Similarly for $\dfrac{d^2u}{d\eta^2}$ and $\dfrac{d^2u}{d\zeta^2}$,

also

$$\frac{d^2u}{d\xi\,d\eta} = -a_1b_1\frac{d^2z}{dx^2} - a_2b_2\frac{d^2z}{dy^2} - (a_1b_2 + a_2b_1)\frac{d^2z}{dx\,dy} = a_3b_3\,r.$$

Similarly for $\dfrac{d^2u}{d\xi\,d\zeta}$ and $\dfrac{d^2u}{d\eta\,d\zeta}$.

Hence differentiating the equation

$$\frac{du}{d\xi} + \frac{du}{d\zeta^2}\frac{d\zeta}{d\xi} = 0,$$

with regard to ξ and substituting we obtain, remembering that

$$\frac{d\zeta}{d\xi} = -\frac{a_3}{c_3}, \quad \text{and } \frac{d\zeta}{d\eta} = -\frac{b_3}{c_3},$$

$$c_3 \cdot \frac{d^2\zeta}{d\xi^2} = (1-a_3^2)\,r + 2a_3^2\,r + (1-c_3^2)\frac{a_3^2}{c_3^2}r = \frac{a_3^2 + c_3^2}{c_3^2}r;$$

$$\therefore\ c_3 \frac{d^2\zeta}{d\xi^2} = \frac{a_3^2 + c_3^2}{c_3^2} r = \left\{1 + \left(\frac{d\zeta}{d\xi}\right)^2\right\} r.$$

Similarly, we should find

$$c_3 \frac{d^2\zeta}{d\eta^2} = \left\{1 + \left(\frac{d\zeta}{d\eta}\right)^2\right\} r,$$

and

$$c_3 \frac{d^2\zeta}{d\xi\, d\eta} = \frac{d\zeta}{d\xi} \cdot \frac{d\zeta}{d\eta} r,$$

whence the proposition is proved.

v. If the differential equations of the first order

$$\phi\left(x, y, \frac{dy}{dx}\right) = a, \qquad \psi\left(x, y, \frac{dy}{dx}\right) = b,$$

give rise to the same differential equation of the second order, shew how the general solution of an equation of the form

$$F\left\{\phi\left(x, y, \frac{dy}{dx}\right),\ \psi\left(x, y, \frac{dy}{dx}\right)\right\} = 0,$$

may be found without integration.

Apply this or any other method to the discovery of the general solution of the equation

$$x^3 y \left(\frac{dy}{dx}\right)^2 + (a^4 - 2x^2 y^2) \frac{dy}{dx} + xy^3 = 0.$$

Here

$$2x^2 y^2 - \frac{xy^3}{p} - x^3 yp = a^4;$$

$$\therefore\ xy \left(x - \frac{y}{p}\right)(y - px) = a^4.$$

But

$$x\left(x - \frac{y}{p}\right) = c, \quad \text{and } y(y - px) = b,$$

give rise to the same differential equation of the 2nd order.

Now

$$p = \frac{1}{x}\left(y - \frac{b}{y}\right) = \frac{xy}{x^2 - c};$$

$$\therefore (y^2 - b)(x^2 - c) = x^2 y^2,$$

$$bx^2 + cy^2 = bc,$$

$$bx^2 + \frac{a^4}{b} y^2 = a^4.$$

6. Enunciate and explain D'Alembert's principle. Apply it to determine the small oscillations in space of a uniform heavy rod of length $2a$, suspended from a fixed point by an inextensible string of length l fastened to one extremity. Prove that, if x be one of the horizontal co-ordinates of that extremity of the rod to which the string is fastened,

$$x = A \sin(n_1 t + \alpha) + B \sin(n_2 t + \beta),$$

where n_1, n_2 are the two positive roots of the equation,

$$aln^4 - (4a + 3l)gn^2 + 3g^2 = 0,$$

and A, B, α, β, are arbitrary constants.

Take O the point of suspension of the string for origin, and the axis of z vertically downwards. Let p, q, p', q' be the cosines of the angles made by the string and rod respectively with the axes of x and y, and let u be the distance of any element du of the rod from that extremity to which the string is attached. Then the co-ordinates of this element will be

$$\left.\begin{array}{l} x = lp + up', \\ y = lq + uq', \\ z = l + u, \end{array}\right\} \quad \dots\dots\dots\dots\dots\dots\dots\dots (1).$$

Then the equations of motion will be

$$\left.\begin{array}{l} l\dfrac{d^2 p}{dt^2} + a\dfrac{d^2 p'}{dt^2} = -\dfrac{Tp}{m}, \\[6pt] l\dfrac{d^2 q}{dt^2} + a\dfrac{d^2 q'}{dt^2} = -\dfrac{Tq}{m}, \\[6pt] 0 = g - \dfrac{T}{m}, \end{array}\right\} \quad \dots\dots\dots\dots(2),$$

where T is the tension of the string and m the mass of the rod. By D'Alembert's principle, the equation of moments round x will be

$$\Sigma \delta u \left(y \frac{d^2 z}{dt^2} - z \frac{d^2 y}{dt^2} \right) = \Sigma \delta u \, (yg),$$

which becomes by (1)

$$\int_0^a du \left\{ -(l+u) \left(l \frac{d^2 q}{dt^2} + u \frac{d^2 q'}{dt^2} \right) \right\} = 2ag \, (lq + aq'),$$

or $-2al \left(l \dfrac{d^2 q}{dt^2} + u \dfrac{d^2 q'}{dt^2} \right) - 2la^2 \dfrac{d^2 q}{dt^2} - \dfrac{8a^3}{3} \dfrac{d^2 q'}{dt^2} = 2ag \, (lq + aq'),$

which by equation (2) reduces to

$$l \frac{d^2 q}{dt^2} + \frac{4}{3} a \frac{d^2 q'}{dt^2} = -gq'.$$

Therefore the four equations of motion are

$$\left. \begin{array}{l} l \dfrac{d^2 p}{dt^2} + a \dfrac{d^2 p'}{dt^2} = -gp, \\[1em] l \dfrac{d^2 p}{dt^2} + \dfrac{4}{3} a \dfrac{d^2 p'}{dt^2} = -gp', \end{array} \right\}$$

and two similar equations for q, q'.

To solve these put

$$p = A \sin(nt + a), \quad q = B \sin(nt + a),$$

we get

$$\left. \begin{array}{l} ln^2 A + an^2 B = gA, \\[0.5em] ln^2 A + \dfrac{4}{3} an^2 B = gB; \end{array} \right\}$$

$$\therefore n^4 - \frac{4a + 3l}{al} g \cdot n^2 + \frac{3g^2}{al} = 0,$$

and the values of n are found.

vii. A rigid body is rotating about an axis through its centre of gravity when a certain point of the body becomes suddenly fixed, the axis being simultaneously set free; find the equations of the new instantaneous axis; and prove that, if it be parallel to the originally fixed axis, the point must lie in the line represented by the equations

$$a^2 lx + b^2 my + c^2 nz = 0,$$

$$(b^2 - c^2)\frac{x}{l} + (c^2 - a^2)\frac{y}{m} + (a^2 - b^2)\frac{z}{n} = 0;$$

the principal axes through the centre of gravity being taken as axes of co-ordinates, a, b, c the radii of gyration about these lines, and l, m, n the direction-cosines of the originally fixed axis referred to them.

In order that the new instantaneous axis may be parallel to the originally fixed axis the plane passing through the impulse at the fixed point and the centre of gravity must be diametral to the originally fixed axis. Hence the point must lie in the plane

$$a^2 lx + b^2 my + c^2 nz = 0 \dots\dots\dots\dots\dots(1).$$

Again, in order that rotation round the original axis through the centre of gravity combined with a velocity of translation parallel to the blow may reduce the point to rest, the line joining the point with the centre of gravity must coincide with the projection of the axis upon the diametral plane; let λ, μ, ν be the direction-cosines of the normal to the plane passing through the axis and the normal to the diametral plane, then

$$l\lambda + m\mu + n\nu = 0,$$

$$a^2 l\lambda + b^2 m\mu + c^2 n\nu = 0,$$

$$l\lambda(c^2 - a^2) + m\mu(c^2 - b^2) = 0, \text{ and so on;}$$

therefore the equation to the plane is

$$(b^2 - c^2)\frac{x}{l} + (c^2 - a^2)\frac{y}{m} + (a^2 - b^2)\frac{z}{n} = 0 \dots\dots(2);$$

(1) and (2) determine the line in which the point must be situated.

ix. Prove the following relation between the perturbations of a planet in longitude and radius vector:

$$\delta\theta = \frac{1}{h}\left\{\frac{d\,(2r\delta r)}{dt} - \frac{1}{r}\frac{dr}{dt}r\delta r + 3\iint\frac{d\,(R)}{dt}dt^2 + 2\int r\frac{dR}{dr}dt\right\},$$

h being twice the sectorial area described in a unit of time by the undisturbed planet round the Sun; and find the corresponding relation whatever be the law of force, provided it be central and a function of the distance only, and provided such a function as R can be found.

Let F be the central force.

Our equations of motion give us

$$\left(\frac{dr}{dt}\right)^2 + r^2\left(\frac{d\theta}{dt}\right)^2 = 2\int F dr - 2\int\frac{d\,(R)}{dt}dt,$$

$$\frac{d^2\,(r^2)}{dt^2} = 4\int F dr - 4\int\frac{d\,(R)}{dt} + 2Fr - 2r\frac{dR}{dr},$$

whence, proceeding as in Airy's *Tracts*, we get

$$3\left(\frac{dr}{dt}\right)^2 + 4r\frac{d^2r}{dt^2} - r^2\left(\frac{d\theta}{dt}\right)^2 = 6\int F dr + 4Fr - 6\int\frac{d\,(R)}{dt}dt - 4r\frac{dR}{dr};$$

put $r + \delta r$, $\theta + \delta\theta$, for r and θ respectively, r and θ being the functions of t given in the undisturbed motion, and we obtain

$$6\frac{dr}{dt}\cdot\frac{d\delta r}{dt} + 4\,\delta r\cdot\frac{d^2r}{dt^2} + 4r\frac{d^2.\,\delta r}{dt^2} - 2r\,\delta r\left(\frac{d\theta}{dt}\right)^2 - 2r^2\frac{d\theta}{dt}\cdot\frac{d\delta\theta}{dt}$$

$$= 6F\delta r + 4F\delta r + 4r\frac{dF}{dr}\delta r - 6\int\frac{d\,(R)}{dt}dt - 4r\frac{dR}{dr},$$

which, as in Airy's *Tracts*, is easily reduced to

$$\frac{d}{dt}\left(4r\frac{d\delta r}{dt} + 2\frac{dr}{dt}\delta r\right) - 2r^2\frac{d\theta}{dt}\cdot\frac{d\delta\theta}{dt}$$

$$= 8\,F\delta r + 4r\frac{dF}{dr}\delta r - 6\int\frac{d\,(R)}{dt}dt - 4r\frac{dR}{dr}.$$

Put h for $r^2 \dfrac{d\theta}{dt}$, and we get

$$\delta\theta = \frac{1}{h}\left\{\frac{d}{dt}(2r\delta r) - \frac{1}{r}\frac{dr}{dt}\cdot r\delta r\right.$$

$$\left. + 3\int\frac{d(R)}{dt}dt + 2r\frac{dR}{dr} - 4F\delta r - 2r\frac{dF}{dr}\delta r\right\}.$$

This is reduced to the equation in the question when F is such a function of r that

$$2F + r\frac{dF}{dr} = 0,$$

or $\qquad\qquad F = \dfrac{\mu}{r^2}.$

10. If the object-glass of a telescope be covered over by a diaphragm, pierced in the centre by a small hole, the form of which is a rectangle, state generally the nature of the spectra formed about the image of a star on a screen placed at the focus.

If the hole be circular and the screen be pushed towards the lens, prove that, when the light is homogeneous, the centre is alternately bright and dark. Trace also the order of the colours seen if the light be not homogeneous.

This rider is obviously the same as the problem solved by Airy in Art. 79 of his Tract on Light. For the introduction of the lens is merely making the incident pencil convergent instead of divergent, that is, the a in Airy's investigation is to be made negative. The intensity of the illumination will be

$$\frac{4\lambda^2 a^2 b^2}{(a-b)^2}\sin^2\left(\frac{2\pi}{\lambda}\frac{a-b}{4ab}c^2\right).$$

The interpretation of this result is nearly the same as that given by Airy, except that we now begin at the central spot.

When $b=a$, the intensity becomes $\pi^2 c^4$; when $b-a = \pm \dfrac{a^2\lambda}{c^2}$, the sine is unity, and intensity is measured by $4c^4$; when $b-a = \pm \dfrac{2a^2\lambda}{c^2}$, the intensity is zero, and as $b-a$ continues to increase, we have alternately brightness and darkness.

If the light be not homogeneous, we have, when $b = a$, a white spot, and as $b - a$ increases; the violet disappears first, leaving a red spot, which gives place to the other colours in order.

FRIDAY, *Jan.* 20.   9 *to* 12.

SENIOR MODERATOR.   Roman numbers.
SENIOR EXAMINER.   Arabic numbers.

1. OA, OB are common tangents to two conics having a common focus S, CA, CB are tangents at one of their points of intersection, BD, AE tangents intersecting CA, CB in D, E. Prove that SDE is a straight line.

Let the conics be reciprocated into two circles within both of which S lies. Fig. 51.

oa, ob, their points of intersection, correspond to OA, OB; ca, cb, the points of contact of a common tangent, to CA, CB.

The straight line b joining cb and ob meets one circle in bd,

.... a ...... ca ... oa ...... the other in ae,

bd, ae correspond to BD, AE,

and d, e which join bd, ca and ae, cb to D and E.

It is required to shew that d, e are parallel.

The angle between d and a = that between b and o = that between a and e.

ii. Define the term potential of a mass, the particles of which attract according to the law of nature; and prove that, if a body moveable about a fixed axis be subject to the action of an attracting mass of which the potential is V, then

$\iiint \dfrac{dV}{d\theta} dm$ is the moment which must be impressed upon the body about that axis in order to produce equilibrium, where θ is the inclination of the plane through the fixed axis and the particle of which the mass is dm to a fixed plane.

A uniform straight line, the particles of which attract according to the law of the inverse square, acts upon a rigid uniform circular arc in the same plane with the line, of which the radius is equal to the line, and which is moveable about an axis through its centre perpendicular to its plane, the axis being coincident with one extremity of the line. Prove that the moment necessary to produce equilibrium when the bounding radii are inclined at the angles α and β to the line produced is proportional to

$$\log \dfrac{\sec \dfrac{\alpha}{2} + 1}{\sec \dfrac{\beta}{2} + 1}.$$

Let AB be the straight line, P a point at a distance r from AB, Fig. 52,

Q a point in the line at dist. x from B,

$$PQ^2 = x^2 + r^2 + 2xr \cos\theta;$$

$$\therefore V = \int_0^r \dfrac{dx}{\sqrt{\{(x + r\cos\theta)^2 + r^2 \sin^2\theta\}}}$$

$$= \log \dfrac{\sqrt{2}\sqrt{(1 + \cos\theta)} + (1 + \cos\theta)}{1 + \cos\theta}$$

$$= \log \dfrac{2\cos\dfrac{\theta}{2} + 2\cos^2\dfrac{\theta}{2}}{2\cos^2\dfrac{\theta}{2}} = \log \dfrac{1 + \cos\dfrac{\theta}{2}}{\cos\dfrac{\theta}{2}} = \log\left(\sec\dfrac{\theta}{2} + 1\right).$$

Hence since in this case $dm = r d\theta$, the moment on

$$\iiint \dfrac{dV}{d\theta} \cdot dm = V_\alpha - V_\beta \propto \log \dfrac{\sec \dfrac{\alpha}{2} + 1}{\sec \dfrac{\beta}{2} + 1}.$$

4. If an elastic string, whose natural length is that of a uniform rod, be attached to the rod at both ends and suspended by the middle point, prove by means of Vis Viva that the rod will sink until the strings are inclined to the horizon at an angle θ, which satisfies the equation

$$\cot^3 \frac{\theta}{2} - \cot \frac{\theta}{2} - 2n = 0,$$

where the tension of the string, when stretched to double its length, is n times the weight.

If the string be suspended by a point, not in the middle, write down the equation of Vis Viva.

C is the point of suspension. Fig. 53.

$ABC = \theta$ at time t.

Let $AB = 2a$, $BC = r = a \sin \theta$,

m the mass of the rod.

The moving effect of the tension of CB

$$= nmg \cdot \frac{r-a}{a}.$$

By Vis Viva, at the time t,

$$mv^2 = 2mga \tan \theta - 4 \int nmg \frac{r-a}{a} dr$$

$$= 2mga \tan \theta - 2nmg \cdot \frac{(r-a)^2}{a},$$

since $v = 0$ when $\theta = 0$, and $r = a$;

therefore the rod comes to rest when

$$\tan \theta - n (\sec \theta - 1)^2 = 0,$$

or $$\sin \theta \cos \theta - 4n \sin^4 \frac{\theta}{2} = 0,$$

or $$\cot^3 \frac{\theta}{2} - \cot \frac{\theta}{2} - 2n = 0.$$

If the fixed point divide the string into the portions $a-c$, $a+c$, and these be inclined at angles θ, θ' to the horizon, and be of length r, r' at the time t, ϕ the inclination of the rod, the equation of Vis Viva gives

$$m\left(\frac{dr}{dt}\right)^2 + mk^2\left(\frac{d\phi}{dt}\right)^2 = 2mgz - nmg\left\{\frac{(r-a+c)^2}{a} + \frac{(r'-a-c)^2}{a}\right\},$$

where $\quad z = \tfrac{1}{2}(r\sin\theta + r'\sin\theta')$,

and $\quad 2a\cos\phi = r\cos\theta + r'\cos\theta'$,

$\quad\quad\quad 2a\sin\phi = -r\sin\theta + r'\cos\theta'$,

which with two more dynamical equations are sufficient to determine the problem of the motion.

5. If an oblate spheroid be moveable about its centre, and θ be the inclination of its equator to a fixed plane, ψ the inclination of the line of intersection of its equator with this plane to a fixed line in the plane, A and C the respective moments of inertia about the axis of figure and a line in the equator respectively, L and M the moments of impressed couples about the line of intersection of the equator with the fixed plane, and a line in the equator perpendicular to this latter line respectively, ω the angular velocity about the axis of figure, prove that

$$C\frac{d^2\theta}{dt^2} - C\left(\frac{d\psi}{dt}\right)^2 \sin\theta\cos\theta + A\omega\sin\theta\frac{d\psi}{dt} = L,$$

$$C\frac{d}{dt}\left(\frac{d\psi}{dt}\sin\theta\right) + C\frac{d\psi}{dt}\frac{d\theta}{dt}\cos\theta - A\omega\frac{d\theta}{dt} = M,$$

hence deduce the precessional and nutational velocity of the Earth's axis, assuming the effect of the Sun's action to be a couple of which the moment is $m\sin\Delta\cos\Delta$ about an axis in the equator $90°$ distant from the Sun, m being a very small quantity, A and C very nearly equal, and the Sun's motion in declination and right ascension being neglected.

The angular velocities about the axis of figure, the line of nodes, and the axis in the equator $90°$ distant from the line of nodes respectively, are

$$\omega, \quad \frac{d\theta}{dt}, \quad \text{and} \quad \frac{d\psi}{dt}\sin\theta,$$

and the line of nodes recedes from the axis of figure with the angular velocity $\frac{d\psi}{dt} \sin \theta$, and approaches the perpendicular to the line of nodes in the equator with the angular velocity $\frac{d\psi}{dt} \cos \theta$. Similarly the perpendicular to the line of nodes in the equator approaches the axis with the angular velocity $\frac{d\theta}{dt}$, and recedes from the line of nodes with the velocity $\frac{d\psi}{dt} \cos \theta$.

Hence by the formulæ for accelerations of angular momenta referred to moving axes,

$$C\frac{d^2\theta}{dt^2} - \frac{d\psi}{dt}\cos\theta \cdot C\frac{d\psi}{dt}\sin\theta + \frac{d\psi}{dt}\sin\theta \cdot A\omega$$

= acceleration of momentum round the line of nodes,

$$C\frac{d}{dt}\cdot\left(\frac{d\psi}{dt}\sin\theta\right) + \frac{d\psi}{dt}\cos\theta \cdot C\frac{d\theta}{dt} - \frac{d\theta}{dt}\cdot A\omega$$

= acceleration of momentum round the axis perpendicular to the line of nodes,

whence the equations in the question.

In the case of the Sun's action upon the Earth

$$L = m \sin \Delta \cos \Delta \sin \alpha,$$
$$M = -m \sin \Delta \cos \Delta \cos \alpha,$$

and the squares of the very small quantities $\frac{d\psi}{dt}$ and $\frac{d\theta}{dt}$ are to be neglected as well as the differencee between A and C.

Hence the equations become

$$\frac{d^2\theta}{dt^2} + \omega \cdot \sin\theta \frac{d\psi}{dt} = \frac{m}{C} \sin\Delta \cos\Delta \sin\alpha,$$

$$\frac{d}{dt}\cdot\left(\sin\theta\frac{d\psi}{dt}\right) - \omega\frac{d\theta}{dt} = -\frac{m}{C}\sin\Delta \cos\Delta \cos\alpha,$$

differentiate the first and subtract the second multiplied by ω, remembering that Δ and α are to be considered constant, and we have

$$\frac{d^2\theta}{dt^2} + \omega^2 \frac{d\theta}{dt} = \frac{m}{C} \omega \sin \Delta \cos \Delta \cos \alpha,$$

$$\frac{d^2}{dt^2} \cdot \left(\frac{d\theta}{dt}\right) + \omega^2 \frac{d\theta}{dt} = \frac{m}{C} \omega \sin \Delta \cos \Delta \cos \alpha;$$

$$\therefore \frac{d\theta}{dt} = \frac{m}{\omega C} \sin \Delta \cos \Delta \cos \alpha.$$

Similarly,

$$\sin \theta \frac{d\psi}{dt} = \frac{m}{\omega C} \sin \Delta \cos \Delta \sin \alpha,$$

neglecting the arbitrary parts of the respective integrals.

6. If a solid of revolution be immersed in a heavy homogeneous fluid with its axis vertical, prove that, when the total normal pressure on the surface is a minimum, its form must be such that the numerical value of the diameter of curvature of the meridian at any point is a harmonic mean between the segments of the normal to the surface at that point intercepted between the point and the surface of the fluid and between the point and the axis, respectively.

In this case $\int xy\, ds$ is to be a minimum.

Hence we must substitute xy for μ in the formula,

$$\frac{1}{\rho} = -\frac{1}{\mu}\left(\frac{d\mu}{dx}\cos\alpha + \frac{d\mu}{dy}\cos\beta\right),$$

giving us

$$-\frac{1}{\rho} = \frac{\cos\alpha}{x} + \frac{\cos\beta}{y}$$

$$-\frac{2}{2\rho} = \frac{1}{x\sec\alpha} + \frac{1}{y\sec\beta},$$

proving the proposition.

viii. Explain the phenomenon of external conical refraction where a small pencil of light passes through a biaxal crystal; and describe an experiment by which this phenomenon may be manifested.

If the crystal be bounded by planes perpendicular to the line bisecting the acute angles between the optic axes, write down equations whence the equation of the cone of emerging rays may be obtained.

Let l, m, n be the direction-cosines of the perpendicular to any wave-front incident upon the second surface of the crystal; the axes of reference being the axes of elasticity; let λ, μ, ν be the direction-cosines of the perpendicular to the corresponding wave-front after emergence. Then λ, μ, ν are the direction-cosines to the corresponding emergent ray, and if the point of the second surface at which the light emerges be taken as origin, the equation of the cone will be determined by eliminating λ, μ, ν between the equations

$$\frac{x}{\lambda} = \frac{y}{\mu} = \frac{z}{\nu} \quad\quad\quad (A),$$

and an equation between λ, μ, ν which remains to be found.

(1) The emergent ray, the normal at the point of emergence and the perpendicular to the front of the incident wave, lie in the same plane, whence

$$\frac{\mu}{\nu} = \frac{m}{n} \quad\quad\quad (B).$$

(2) The sines of the angles of emergence and incidence are to each other as $u : v$, u being taken for the velocity of light in air, and v for the velocity with which the wave-front under consideration was propagated through the crystal, whence

$$\frac{1-\lambda^2}{u^2} = \frac{1-l^2}{v^2} \quad\quad\quad (C).$$

(3) Also the value of v in terms of l, m, n is to be found by substituting the values corresponding to the multiple point in the equations α (page 18 of Griffin's tract on Double Refraction), whence we obtain the following relations,

$$\left. \begin{array}{c} \dfrac{v^2-a^2}{\sqrt{\{(a^2-c^2)(a^2-b^2)\}}} = \mp \dfrac{vl}{c} \\ \dfrac{v^2-c^2}{\sqrt{\{(a^2-c^2)(b^2-c^2)\}}} = \pm \dfrac{vn}{a} \end{array} \right\} \quad\quad (D).$$

Between the four equations of B, C, and D, and the additional equation

$$l^2 + m^2 + n^2 = 1,$$

we may eliminate l, m, n, and v, and obtain the relation sought between λ, μ, and ν.

The final relation between x, y, and z gives a cone of the fourth degree.

FRIDAY, *Jan.* 20. 1½ *to* 4.

JUNIOR MODERATOR.   Roman numbers.
JUNIOR EXAMINER.   Arabic numbers.

1. IF α, β, γ be the respective distances of a straight line from the three angular points of a triangle ABC, these distances being reckoned positive or negative according as their directions fall within the angles of the triangle itself or their supplements, investigate the following relation,

$(\alpha \sin A)^2 + (\beta \sin B)^2 + (\gamma \sin C)^2 - 2 \cos A \sin B \sin C \beta \gamma$

$- 2 \cos B \sin C \sin A \gamma\alpha - 2 \cos C \sin A \sin B \alpha\beta$

$= 4R^2 \sin^2 A \sin^2 B \sin^2 C,$

where R is the radius of the circumscribed circle.

Referring to fig. 54, we have

$$AP = \alpha, \quad BQ = -\beta, \quad CR = -\gamma.$$

Hence, if $BC = a$, $CA = b$, $AB = c$, and $BAP = \dfrac{A}{2} - \theta$,

$$A\gamma = \alpha + \beta = c \cos\left(\dfrac{A}{2} - \theta\right),$$

similarly $\qquad \alpha + \gamma = b \cos\left(\dfrac{A}{2} + \theta\right);$

I.

$$\therefore b(\alpha+\beta)+c(\alpha+\gamma) = 2bc\cos\frac{A}{2}\cos\theta,$$

$$b(\alpha+\beta)+c(\alpha+\gamma) = 2bc\sin\frac{A}{2}\sin\theta.$$

Multiply these by $\sin\frac{A}{2}$, $\cos\frac{A}{2}$, respectively, and add squares, then, since $bc\sin A = \frac{abc}{2R}$,

$$b^2(\alpha+\beta)^2 + c^2(\alpha+\gamma)^2 - 2bc\cos A(\alpha+\beta)(\alpha+\gamma) = \frac{a^2b^2c^2}{4R^2},$$

or, since $2bc\cos A = b^2 + c^2 - a^2$,

$$a^2\alpha^2 + b^2\beta^2 + c^2\gamma^2 - 2bc\cos A\cdot\beta\gamma - 2ca\cos B\cdot\gamma\alpha$$
$$- 2ab\cos C\cdot\alpha\beta = \frac{a^2b^2c^2}{4R^2}.$$

Now, $\quad\dfrac{\sin A}{a} = \dfrac{\sin B}{b} = \dfrac{\sin C}{c} = \dfrac{1}{2R};$

$\therefore (\alpha\sin A)^2 + (\beta\sin B)^2 + (\gamma\sin C)^2 - 2\cos A\sin B\sin C\cdot\beta\gamma$

$- 2\cos B\sin C\sin A\cdot\gamma\alpha - 2\cos C\sin A\sin B\cdot\alpha\beta$

$$= 4R\sin^2 A\sin^2 B\sin^2 C,$$

the required result.

2. State the positive and negative characteristics of a singular solution of a differential equation; and shew how it is deduced from the complete primitive. Shew also how the singular solution of a differential equation of the first order is obtained from the equation itself.

Obtain the singular solution of the equation of which

$$y\cos^2 m = 2\cos(x - 2m)$$

is the complete primitive; and find the singular solution of the equation

$$(x+y)^2\left(\frac{dy}{dx}\right)^3 - (x^2-y^2)\left(\frac{dy}{dx}\right)^2 + 1 = 0.$$

(α) $y \cos^2 m = 2 \cos(x - 2m)$.

This may be put into the form
$$(y - \cos x) \cos 2m - \sin x \sin 2m = \frac{y}{2}.$$

Differentiating with respect to m, we get
$$(y - \cos x) \sin 2m + \sin x \cos 2m = 0,$$
whence, adding squares and reducing,
$$\frac{3y^2}{4} - 2y \cos x + 1 = 0,$$
the required singular solution.

(β) This may be written under the form
$$(x + y)^3 p^3 - (x^2 - y^2) p^2 + 1 = 0.$$
The condition for a singular solution is
$$\frac{dp}{dy} = \infty,$$
which, in this case, gives
$$3(x + y)^3 p^2 - 2(x^2 - y^2) p = 0,$$
$$\text{or} \quad p = \frac{2}{3} \frac{x - y}{(x + y)^2}.$$

Substituting this value for p in the original equation, we get
$$\frac{8}{27} \left(\frac{x - y}{x + y}\right)^3 - \frac{4}{9} \left(\frac{x - y}{x + y}\right)^2 + 1 = 0,$$
$$\text{or} \quad 4(x - y)^3 = 27(x + y)^2,$$
the required singular solution.

iii. Prove that, in any curve of double curvature, the locus of the centres of spherical curvature is the edge of regression of the envelope of the normal planes. Prove also that this locus cannot be an evolute.

The normal plane to the locus of the centres of circular curvature bisects the radius of spherical curvature.

If two consecutive normal planes be drawn to a curve, their intersection is a generator of the envelope of the planes, or, as it is usually called, of the polar surface. The envelope of these generators is known to be the edge of regression, that is, any two consecutive generators intersect on the edge of regression.

The intersection of two consecutive normal planes is a straight line through the centre of circular curvature, and it is clearly such that if any point be taken on it, that point is equally distant from three consecutive points on the curve. Therefore the intersection of two consecutive generators is equally distant from four consecutive points on the curve, i.e. it is the centre of spherical curvature.

Hence the proposition follows.

It is also clear that the edge of regression cannot be an evolute, because its tangents, which are the generators of the above polar surface, do not pass through the original curve.

Let A, A', A'' be three consecutive points on a curve, and let the plane of the paper be the normal plane at A'. Let CO be the intersection of the normal planes at A, A'; $C'O$ the intersection of those at A', A''. Let the plane that passes through the three points A, A', A'' cut CO, $C'O$ in C and C'. Then C, C' are ultimately two consecutive centres of circular curvature, and O is the corresponding centre of spherical curvature. Fig. 55.

Now $A'CO$, $A'C'O$, are two right angles in one plane, and therefore a circle described on $A'O$ as diameter will pass through C and C'. And CC' is ultimately a tangent to the circle, hence a normal to CC' bisects $A'O$ the diameter. But CC' is also ultimately a tangent to the locus of C, whence the normal plane to the locus of C bisects $A'O$ the radius of spherical curvature.

4. Determine the class of curves which possess the property that the locus of the extremity of the polar subtangent of any one is similar to the curve itself.

Shew that $r\theta\epsilon^{m\theta} = a$ is the equation of such a curve.

It may be shewn that, if $\frac{1}{r} = f(\theta)$ be the equation of a given curve, that of the locus of the extremity of its polar subtangent is $\frac{1}{r} = f'\left(\theta - \frac{\pi}{2}\right)$.

Now, if $\quad f(\theta) = \dfrac{\theta \epsilon^{m\theta}}{a}$,

$$f'\left(\theta - \frac{\pi}{2}\right) = \frac{m\left(\theta - \dfrac{\pi}{2}\right) + 1}{a} \epsilon^{m\left(\theta - \frac{\pi}{2}\right)}$$

$$= \frac{1}{a\epsilon}\left\{m\left(\theta - \frac{\pi}{2}\right) + 1\right\} \epsilon^{m\left(\theta - \frac{\pi}{2}\right)+1}.$$

Hence, the equation of the locus of the extremities of the polar subtangents of the curve $r\theta\epsilon^{m\theta} = a$, is

$$r\left(\theta - \frac{\pi}{2} + \frac{1}{m}\right) \epsilon^{m\left(\theta - \frac{\pi}{2} + \frac{1}{m}\right)} = \frac{\epsilon}{m} a,$$

representing a curve of similar form to the given one, but with its dimensions varied in the ratio $\epsilon : m$, and turned through an angle $\dfrac{\pi}{2} - \dfrac{1}{m}$.

v. If a homogeneous sphere roll on a perfectly rough plane under the action of any forces whatever, of which the resultant passes through the centre of the sphere, the motion of the centre of gravity will be the same as if the plane were smooth and all the forces were reduced in a certain constant ratio; and the plane is the only surface which possesses this property.

Take the plane as the plane of xy, and take axes fixed in space. Let $\omega_1, \omega_2, \omega_3$ be the angular velocities about diameters parallel to the axes. Let v_x, v_y, v_z be the velocities of the centre, X, Y, Z the impressed forces, and F, G the frictions resolved parallel to the axes. Let $a =$ radius of the sphere. Then the equations of motion will be

$$\kappa^2 \frac{d\omega_1}{dt} = Ga,$$

$$\kappa^2 \frac{d\omega_2}{dt} = -Fa, \quad \quad \quad \quad \quad (1)$$

$$\kappa^2 \frac{d\omega_3}{dt} = 0,$$

$$\frac{dv_x}{dt} = X + F,$$

$$\frac{dv_y}{dt} = Y + G, \quad \quad \quad \quad \quad (2)$$

and since the point of contact is at rest we have the geometrical equations

$$v_x - a\omega_2 = 0,$$
$$v_y + a\omega_1 = 0. \quad \quad \quad \quad \quad (3)$$

By differentiating (3) and substituting from (2) we have

$$F = -\frac{\kappa^2}{a^2} \frac{dv_x}{dt},$$

$$G = -\frac{\kappa^2}{a^2} \frac{dv_y}{dt}.$$

Hence the equations of motion of the centre are

$$\frac{dv_x}{dt} = \frac{a^2}{a^2 + \kappa^2} X,$$

$$\frac{dv_y}{dt} = \frac{a^2}{a^2 + \kappa^2} Y.$$

These are the very equations we should have had if the plane had been smooth and forces had been reduced in the ratio $\frac{a^2}{a^2 + \kappa^2}$.

A rough plane is the only surface which possesses the property enunciated in the question.

Let l, m, n be the direction-cosines of the normal at any point of a surface, X', Y', Z' the resolved parts of the friction, and v_x, v_y, v_z of the velocities of the centre of gravity parallel to the axes. Then by the question

$$X' = -\lambda \frac{dv_x}{dt}, \quad Y' = -\lambda \frac{dv_y}{dt}, \quad Z' = -\lambda \frac{dv_z}{dt}.$$

Also the equations of motion are

$$\left.\begin{aligned}\kappa^2 \frac{d\omega_x}{dt} &= (mZ' - nY')a, \\ \kappa^2 \frac{d\omega_y}{dt} &= (nX' - lZ')a, \\ \kappa^2 \frac{d\omega_z}{dt} &= (lY' - mX')a,\end{aligned}\right\}$$

and the geometrical equations are

$$\left.\begin{aligned}v_x &= (\omega_z m - \omega_y n)\, a, \\ v_y &= (\omega_x n - \omega_z l)\, a, \\ v_z &= (\omega_y l - \omega_x m)\, a;\end{aligned}\right\}$$

$$\therefore \frac{\kappa^2}{\lambda} \frac{d\omega_z}{dt} = am \frac{dv_x}{dt} - al \frac{dv_y}{dt}$$

$$= a^2 \frac{d\omega_z}{dt} - na \left(l \frac{d\omega_x}{dt} + m \frac{d\omega_y}{dt} + n \frac{d\omega_z}{dt} \right)$$

$$- \frac{dn}{dt} a \, (l\omega_x + m\omega_y + n\omega_z);$$

$$\therefore \frac{dn}{dt}(l\omega_x + m\omega_y + n\omega_z) = \mu \frac{d\omega_z}{dt},$$

where μ is a constant, also

$$\frac{dl}{dt}(l\omega_x + m\omega_y + n\omega_z) = \mu \frac{d\omega_x}{dt},$$

$$\frac{dm}{dt}(l\omega_x + m\omega_y + n\omega_z) = \mu \frac{d\omega_y}{dt},$$

Multiply these by ω_x, ω_x, ω_y and add, we get, since

$$l\frac{d\omega_x}{dt} + m\frac{d\omega_y}{dt} + n\frac{d\omega_z}{dt} = 0,$$

$$(l\omega_x + m\omega_y + n\omega_z)^2 = C + \mu(\omega_x^2 + \omega_y^2 + \omega_z^2)$$
$$= C + \mu\Omega^2,$$

where Ω is the resultant of the angular velocities ω_x, ω_y, ω_z.

Now $$lv_x + mv_y + nv_z = 0;$$

$$\therefore v_x\frac{dl}{dt} + v_y\frac{dm}{dt} + v_z\frac{dn}{dt} = 0,$$

and $$l\frac{dl}{dt} + m\frac{dm}{dt} + n\frac{dn}{dt} = 0,$$

by cross-multiplication, we get

$$\therefore \frac{dl}{dt} = P(v_y n - v_z m)$$

$$= Pa^2\{\omega_x - l(l\omega_x + m\omega_y + n\omega_z)\}$$

$$= Pa^2\{\Omega la^2 - l\sqrt{(C + \mu\Omega^2)}\},$$

$$\therefore = Ql \text{ say};$$

$$\therefore \frac{dl}{dt} = Ql, \quad \frac{dm}{dt} = Qm, \quad \frac{dn}{dt} = Qn,$$

whence it easily follows that l, m, n are constants.

vii. If the Earth be completely covered by a sea of small depth, prove that the depth in latitude l is very nearly equal to $H(1 - \epsilon \sin^2 l)$ where H is the depth at the equator, and ϵ the ellipticity of the Earth.

The surface of the Earth and the surface of the water resting on the Earth will both be surfaces of equilibrium, and therefore will be similar spheroids. Draw two parallel tangent planes to the Earth and to the surface of the sea, the distance h between these planes is the depth of the sea at the point at which the tangent planes were drawn. Let p be the perpendicular from the centre on either of these planes, then by similar figures, the ratio $\dfrac{h}{p}$ is constant. Let l be the latitude of the place, a, b the semi-axes of the spheroid, then

$$p^2 = a^2 \cos^2 l + b^2 \sin^2 l$$
$$= a^2(1 - 2\epsilon \sin^2 l);$$
$$\therefore p = a(1 - \epsilon \sin^2 l);$$
$$\therefore h = H(1 - \epsilon \sin^2 l);$$

where H is some constant. But putting $l = 0$, we get $h = H$; therefore H is the depth of the sea at the equator.

ix. The base of an infinite cylinder is the space contained between an equilateral hyperbola and its asymptotes. A plane is drawn perpendicular to the base, and cutting it in a straight line parallel to an asymptote, and the portion of the cylinder between this plane and its parallel asymptote is filled with homogeneous fluid, under the action of no impressed forces. The plane being suddenly removed, determine the motion; and prove that the free surface of the fluid will remain plane, and advance with a uniform velocity proportional to $\sqrt{\varpi}$, where ϖ is the pressure at an infinite distance, which is supposed to remain constant throughout the motion.

Since the fluid starts from rest, the function ϕ exists, and we have

$$\frac{d^2\phi}{dx^2} + \frac{d^2\phi}{dy^2} = 0.$$

Transforming to polar co-ordinates

$$\frac{d}{dr}\left(r\frac{d\phi}{dr}\right) + \frac{1}{r}\frac{d^2\phi}{d\theta^2} = 0.$$

To solve this, assume

$$\phi = Ar^n \epsilon^{m\theta};$$

$$\therefore n^2 + m^2 = 0;$$

$$\therefore \phi = Ar^{\pm n} \cdot \epsilon^{n\theta \sqrt{(-1)}},$$

or generally ϕ can be expressed in a series whose general term is

$$\phi = \left(Ar^n + \frac{B}{r^n}\right) \cos n\theta \quad \ldots \ldots \ldots \ldots (1).$$

The number of terms to be taken and the values of n clearly depend on the geometrical conditions of the bounding surfaces.

Now we know that the curve $\phi =$ constant cuts all the lines of motion at right angles, hence this curve must also cut at right angles the sides of the containing vessel. Let $r'\theta'$ be the co-ordinates of any point of the hyperbola or of its asymptotes, then we must have

$$r^2 + \frac{dr}{d\theta} \cdot \frac{dr'}{d\theta'} = 0 \quad \ldots \ldots \ldots \ldots \ldots (2).$$

The hyperbola and its asymptotes may be included in the single equation $r'^2 \sin 2\theta' = 2a^2$, where a has the two values $a = a$ and $a = 0$.

Hence $\quad\dfrac{dr'}{d\theta'} = -r \cot 2\theta.$

Again, from the value of ϕ we have

$$\Sigma \left(Ar^n - \frac{B}{r^n}\right) \frac{\cos n\theta}{r} \cdot \frac{dr}{d\theta} = \Sigma \left(Ar^n + \frac{B}{r^n}\right) \sin n\theta.$$

Hence equation (2) becomes

$$\Sigma \left(Ar^n - \frac{B}{r^n}\right) \cos n\theta \cdot \tan 2\theta = \Sigma \left(Ar^n + \frac{B}{r^n}\right) \sin n\theta \ldots (3).$$

This equation will evidently be satisfied if we take $n = 2$ and $B = 0$, hence we have

$$\phi = Ar^2 \cos 2\theta \ldots \ldots \ldots \ldots \ldots \ldots (4).$$

This value of ϕ determines the motion, and we shall know that it is the true value if the *other* conditions of the problem are satisfied. These conditions are that the fluid starts from rest, and that along the free surface to be determined from equation (4) the pressure should equal zero.

First, to determine the motion from (4); we have

$$\phi = A(x^2 - y^2);$$

$$\therefore \frac{dx}{dt} = 2Ax, \quad \frac{dy}{dt} = -2Ay,$$

hence the velocity of any particle distant r from the centre is $2Ar$; and all the particles move along hyperbolas having the axes for asymptotes. Take any particle whose co-ordinates are x_0, y_0 at time $t = 0$, its co-ordinates at any other time are

$$x = x_0 \epsilon^{2\int_0^t A\,dt}, \quad y = y_0 \epsilon^{-2\int_0^t A\,dt},$$

hence, if two particles have the same abscissæ at the time $t = 0$, they always have the same abscissæ, and therefore the free boundary of the fluid being originally a straight line, it will be always a straight line.

Secondly, to determine the pressure at any point; we have

$$p = C - \frac{v^2}{2} - \frac{d\phi}{dt} \quad \ldots\ldots\ldots\ldots\ldots\ldots (5).$$

Let ξ, η be the co-ordinates of any point in the free surface of the fluid; then

$$0 = C - 2A^2(\xi^2 + \eta^2) - \frac{dA}{dt}(\xi^2 - \eta^2),$$

or

$$C = \left(2A^2 + \frac{dA}{dt}\right)\xi^2 + \left(2A^2 - \frac{dA}{dt}\right)\eta^2.$$

This by hypothesis is a straight line parallel to the axis of η;

$$\therefore 2A^2 - \frac{dA}{dt} = 0;$$

$$\therefore \frac{1}{A} = \frac{1}{A_0} - 2t,$$

where A_0 is an arbitrary constant;

$$\therefore C = 4A^2\xi^2 = 4\frac{A_0^2 \xi^2}{(1 - 2A_0 t)^2}.$$

The pressure at infinity is $p = \varpi$, and throughout the fluid we have

$$p = C - 4A^2 x^2 \ldots\ldots\ldots\ldots\ldots\ldots(6);$$
$$\therefore \varpi = C,$$

hence along the free surface, equating the two values of C,

$$\xi = -\frac{\sqrt{\omega}}{2A_0} + \sqrt{\omega} t$$
$$= \xi_0 + \sqrt{\omega} t,$$

where ξ_0 is the abscissa of the free surface at the time $t = 0$. Hence the boundary moves uniformly with a velocity $\sqrt{\omega}$.

SENATE-HOUSE PROBLEMS AND RIDERS

FOR THE YEAR EIGHTEEN HUNDRED AND SIXTY.

MODERATORS:

HENRY WILLIAM WATSON, M.A. Trinity College.
EDWARD JOHN ROUTH, M.A. St Peter's College.

EXAMINERS:

PERCIVAL FROST, M.A. St John's College.
NORMAN MACLEOD FERRERS, M.A. Gonville and Caius College.

TUESDAY, *January* 3. 9 to 12.

In the answers to the first six questions the symbol − must not be used. The only abbreviation admitted for the square described on AB is sq. on AB, and for the rectangle contained by AB and CD, the rect. AB, CD.

1. DEFINE parallel straight lines.

Parallelograms upon the same base, and between the same parallels, are equal to one another.

If a straight line DME be drawn through the middle point M of the base BC of a triangle ABC, so as to cut off equal parts AD, AE from the sides AB, AC, produced if necessary respectively, then shall BD be equal to CE.

2. Describe a square that shall be equal to a given rectilineal figure.

Shew how to construct a rectangle which shall be equal to a given square; (1) when the sum, and (2) when the difference of two adjacent sides is given.

3. If, from any point without a circle, two straight lines be drawn, one of which cuts the circle, and the other touches it, the rectangle contained by the whole line which cuts the circle, and

the part of it without the circle, shall be equal to the square on the line which touches it.

If two chords AB, AC be drawn from any point A of a circle, and be produced to D and E, so that the rectangle AC, AE is equal to the rectangle AB, AD, then, if O be the centre of the circle, AO is perpendicular to DE.

iv. Describe an isosceles triangle, having each of the angles at the base double of the third angle.

If A be the vertex, and BD the base of the constructed triangle, D being one of the points of intersection of the two circles employed in the construction, and E the other, and AE be drawn meeting BD produced in F, prove that FAB is another isosceles triangle of the same kind.

v. If the outward angle of a triangle, made by producing one of its sides, be divided into two equal angles by a straight line which also cuts the base produced; the segments between the dividing line and the extremities of the base have the same ratio which the other sides of the triangle have to one another.

If the two sides, containing the angle through which the bisecting line is drawn, be equal, interpret the result of the proposition.

Prove, from this proposition and the preceding, that the straight lines, bisecting one angle of a triangle internally and the other two externally pass through the same point.

vi. If two straight lines be cut by parallel planes, they shall be cut in the same ratio.

If three straight lines, which do not all lie in one plane, be cut in the same ratio by three planes, two of which are parallel, shew that the third will be parallel to the other two, if its intersections with the three straight lines are not all in one straight line.

vii. Define a parabola; and prove, from the definition, that it cannot be cut by a straight line in more than two points.

Prove that, if the tangent at P meet the directrix in D, DSP is a right angle.

viii. If P be a point in an ellipse of which the foci are S and H, the straight line, which bisects the angle between SP produced and HP, meets the ellipse in no point but P.

P, Q are points in two confocal ellipses, at which the line joining the common foci subtends equal angles; prove that the tangents at P, Q are inclined at an angle which is equal to the angle subtended by PQ at either focus.

ix. Assuming the property of the tangent to an ellipse enunciated in 8, prove that $SY \cdot HZ = BC^2$.

If a circle, passing through Y and Z, touch the major axis in Q, and that diameter of the circle, which passes through Q, meet the tangent in P, then $PQ = BC$.

10. Prove that, if in any ellipse any diameter CD be drawn parallel to the tangent at the extremity of any other diameter CP, then CP will also be parallel to the tangent at the extremity of CD.

If PG, the normal at P, cut the major axis in G, and if DR, PN be the ordinates of D and P, prove that the triangles PGN, DRC are similar; and thence deduce that PG bears a constant ratio to CD.

11. Define an asymptote to an hyperbola; and prove that, if from any point in the curve straight lines be drawn parallel to and terminated by the asymptotes, their rectangle is invariable.

In an hyperbola, supposing the two asymptotes and one point of the curve to be given in position, shew how to construct the curve; and find the position of the foci.

12. If a right cone be cut by a plane which is not parallel to a line in the surface, and which meets only one sheet of the cone, the section will be an ellipse.

Given a right cone and a point within it, there are but two sections which have this point for focus; and the planes of these sections make equal angles with the straight line joining the given point and the vertex of the cone.

TUESDAY, *January* 3. $1\frac{1}{2}$ to 4.

1. THE sum of £177 is to be divided among 15 men, 20 women, and 30 children, in such a manner that a man and a child may together receive as much as two women, and all the women may together receive £60; what will they respectively receive?

2. A wine merchant buys 12 dozen of port at 84*s.* per dozen, and 60 dozen more at 48*s.* per dozen; he mixes them, and sells the mixture at 72*s.* per dozen; what profit per cent. does he realize on his original outlay?

3. Assuming that a^m is defined by the equation $a^m \cdot a^n = a^{m+n}$ for all values of m and n, and that $a^1 = a$, interpret the expression a^m, when m is any commensurable quantity, positive or negative. Extend your mode of interpretation, so as to assign a meaning to such a symbol as $a^{\sqrt{2}}$.

4. Solve the equations,

$$\frac{x+2}{3} + \frac{x+3}{2} = x \quad \ldots\ldots\ldots\ldots\ldots\ldots (1),$$

$$\frac{2x + (x^2 - a^2)^{\frac{1}{2}}}{2x - (x^2 - a^2)^{\frac{1}{2}}} + \frac{2x - (x^2 - a^2)^{\frac{1}{2}}}{2x + (x^2 - a^2)^{\frac{1}{2}}} = \frac{3}{2} \quad \ldots\ldots\ldots (2),$$

$$x^2 - yz = a^2, \; y^2 - zx = b^2, \; z^2 - xy = c^2 \ldots\ldots\ldots\ldots (3).$$

5. Explain the terms permutation and combination; and find the number of permutations of n things taken r together.

If $_nP_r$ represent the number of permutations of n things taken r together, and $a_1, a_2, a_3 \ldots$ be the successive terms of a descending arithmetical progression, of which the common difference is d, prove that

$$_{a_1}P_d \cdot {_{a_2}P_d} \cdots {_{a_m}P_d} = {_{a_1}P_{md}}.$$

6. Prove the Binomial Theorem for a positive integral value of the index.

Prove that $2^m - \dfrac{m}{1} 2^{m-1} + \dfrac{m(m-1)}{1 \cdot 2} 2^{m-2} - \ldots + (-1)^m = 1$.

vii. Define a logarithm; and prove that $\log_a N = \log_a b \cdot \log_b N$; and, given that $\log_{10} 2 = \cdot 30103$, find $\log_{25} 50$.

viii. Define the principal trigonometrical ratios; and trace the changes in sign of $\dfrac{\sin(\pi \cos \theta)}{\cos(\pi \sin \theta)}$, as θ varies from 0 to π.

ix. Prove the formula $\sin(A+B) = \sin A \cos B + \cos A \sin B$, A and B being each less than a right angle; and assuming its truth when the values of A and B are unlimited, deduce the expression for $\cos(A-B)$.

x. Prove that

$$\sin A + \sin B = 2 \sin \frac{A+B}{2} \cos \frac{A-B}{2},$$

and $\sin 3(A - 15°) = 4 \cos(A - 45°) \cos(A + 15°) \sin(A - 15°)$, and find $\sin A$ and $\sin B$ from the equations

$$a \sin^2 A + b \sin^2 B = c,$$
$$a \sin 2A - b \sin 2B = 0.$$

xi. Prove, a priori, that $\sin A$, when expressed in terms of $\sin \frac{A}{2}$, has two equal values of opposite signs; and that $\cos A$, when expressed in terms of $\cos \frac{A}{2}$, has only one value; and give a geometrical illustration.

xii. Prove that, when θ is less than $\frac{\pi}{2}$, $\sin \theta$, θ, and $\tan \theta$ are in order of magnitude, and that they vanish in a ratio of equality.

A railway passenger seated in one corner of the carriage looks out of the windows at the further end and observes that a star near the horizon is traversing these windows in the direction of the train's motion and that it is obscured by the partition between the corner window on his own side of the carriage and the middle window while the train is moving through the seventh part of a mile. Shew that the train is on a curve the concavity of which is directed towards the star, and which, if it be circular, has a radius of nearly three miles; the length of the carriage being seven feet and the breadth of the partition four inches.

xiii. If a, b, and B be given, shew under what circumstances there will be two triangles satisfying the conditions of the problem.

Prove that the circles circumscribing both triangles are equal in magnitude, and that the distance between their centres is

$$\sqrt{(b^2 \operatorname{cosec}^2 B - a^2)}.$$

WEDNESDAY, *January* 4. 9 to 12.

1. ENUNCIATE the proposition of the parallelogram of forces; and, assuming its truth for the *magnitude*, prove it also for the *direction*, of the resultant.

2. When three forces acting at a point are in equilibrium, each force is proportional to the sine of the angle between the other two.

Two equal particles, each attracting with a force varying directly as the distance, are situated at the opposite extremities of a diameter of a horizontal circle, on whose circumference a small smooth ring is capable of sliding; prove that the ring will be kept at rest in any position under the attraction of the particles.

3. When three forces, acting in one plane on a rigid body produce equilibrium, the algebraical sum of the moments of either pair about any point in the line of action of the third is zero.

Two equal heavy particles are situated at the extremities of the latus rectum of a parabolic arc without weight, which is placed with its vertex in contact with that of an equal parabola, whose axis is vertical and concavity downwards; prove that the parabolic arc may be turned through any angle without disturbing its equilibrium, provided no sliding be possible between the curves.

4. Find the position of equilibrium when a common balance is loaded with given unequal weights.

If the tongue of the balance be very slightly out of adjustment, prove that the true weight of a body is the arithmetic mean of its apparent weights, when weighed in the opposite scales.

5. Prove that every rigid body has one and only one centre of gravity.

In the figure of Euclid, Book I. Prop. 47, if the perimeters of the squares be regarded as physical lines uniform throughout, prove that the figure will balance about the middle point of the hypothenuse with that line horizontal, the lines of construction having no weight.

6. Enunciate the principal laws of statical friction.

A uniform heavy rod, having one extremity attached to a fixed point, about which it is free to move in all directions, passes over the circumference of a rough ring whose centre is at the fixed point and whose plane is inclined at a given angle to the horizon; find the limiting position of equilibrium.

vii. Explain how uniform velocity and uniform acceleration are measured.

A point, moving with a uniform acceleration, describes 20 feet in the half-second which elapses after the first second of its motion; compare its acceleration with that of a falling heavy particle; and give its numerical measure, taking a minute as the unit of time, and a mile as that of space.

viii. Describe any experiment by which it is shewn, that a force acting on a given particle, produces an acceleration, proportional to the statical measure of the force. Hence deduce a definition of mass.

ix. A heavy particle slides down a smooth inclined plane of given height; prove that the time of its descent varies as the secant of the inclination of the plane to the vertical.

x. Prove that the path of a projectile in a vacuum is a parabola.

A heavy particle is projected from a given point with a given velocity so as to pass through another given point; prove that, in general, there will be two parabolic paths which the particle may describe; and give a geometrical construction to determine their foci. Also find the locus of the second point in order that there may be only one parabolic path.

xi. Two imperfectly elastic balls of given masses, moving in the same directions with given velocities, impinge directly on one another; determine their velocities after impact.

A series of perfectly elastic balls are arranged in the same straight line, one of them impinges directly on the next, and so on; prove that, if their masses form a geometrical progression of which the common ratio is 2, their velocities after impact will form a geometrical progression of which the common ratio is $\frac{2}{3}$.

xii. Define the cycloid; and prove that, if a particle oscillate in a cycloid, the time of an oscillation will be independent of the arc of vibration.

WEDNESDAY, *January* 4. $1\frac{1}{2}$ to 4.

1. EXPLAIN what is meant by "the pressure of a fluid referred to a unit of area." Prove that the pressure at any depth z below the surface of a homogeneous fluid of density ρ, contained in a vessel of any form, may be found from the formula $p = g\rho z + \Pi$, where Π is the pressure of the atmosphere.

A uniform tube is bent into the form of a parabola, and placed with its vertex downwards and axis vertical: supposing any quantities of two fluids of densities ρ, ρ' to be poured into it, and r, r' to be the distances of the two free surfaces respectively, from the focus, then the distance of the common surface from the focus will be $\dfrac{r\rho - r'\rho'}{\rho - \rho'}$.

2. The whole fluid pressure on a surface immersed in a fluid is equal to the weight of a column of fluid, having for base the area of the surface immersed and for height the depth of the centre of gravity of the surface below the surface of the fluid. In what case will this give the resultant pressure?

A parallelogram is immersed in a fluid with one side in the surface; shew how to draw a line from one extremity of this side dividing the parallelogram into two parts on which the pressures are equal.

3. A heavy homogeneous body being wholly immersed in a fluid; shew how to find the magnitude and line of action of the force required to keep it in any given position.

A heavy hollow right cone, closed by a base without weight, is immersed in a fluid, find the force that will sustain it with its axis horizontal.

4. State the law that connects the temperature, density, and elastic force of any gas.

If a quantity of heavy elastic fluid of uniform temperature be placed in a vessel, prove that, if it be divided into indefinitely thin horizontal strata of equal thickness, the densities of the strata will be in geometrical progression.

A given weight of heavy elastic fluid of uniform temperature is confined in a smooth vertical cylinder by a piston of given weight; shew how to find the volume of the fluid.

5. Describe the action of the Fire-engine; and explain the use of the air vessel.

If A be the area of the section of each pump, l the length of the stroke, n the number of strokes per minute, B the area of the hose, find the mean velocity with which the water rushes out.

6. Explain the terms specific gravity and density; and shew how to compare the specific gravities of two fluids by weighing the same body in each.

Supposing some light material, whose density is ρ, to be weighed by means of weights of density ρ', the density of the atmosphere when the barometer stands at 30 inches being unity; shew that, if the mercury in the barometer fall one inch, the material will appear to be altered by $\dfrac{\rho' - \rho}{(\rho - 1)(30\rho' - 29)}$ of its former weight. Will it appear to weigh more or less?

vii. A small convergent pencil of light is incident directly on a concave spherical mirror; investigate the relation between the distances of the conjugate foci from the surface.

If the convergence be measured by the angle of the cone of rays, prove that the convergence of the reflected is greater than that of the incident pencil by a constant quantity.

viii. Find the number of images of a bright point, which can be formed by reflections at two plane mirrors inclined at an angle which is contained an exact number of times in two right angles.

ix. Find the deviation of a ray refracted through a prism in a plane perpendicular to its edge.

A bright point is at the bottom of still water, and an eye is vertically above it, at the same distance from the surface; if a small isosceles prism, of which the refractive angle i is nearly two right angles, be interposed so as to have its base in contact with the water, prove that the angular distance between the images of the point in the two faces is $\dfrac{\mu - 1}{\mu' + 1} (\pi - i)$, μ', μ being the refractive indices for water and for the prism, respectively.

x. Investigate the position of the geometrical focus of a pencil of rays directly refracted through a concave lens of focal length f.

Prove that, as the focus of an incident convergent pencil moves from the lens, the distance between the conjugate foci always increases, except when the focus of incident rays passes between the distances f and $2f$ from the lens.

xi. Describe the eye, regarded as an optical instrument; illustrating the description by drawing pencils from any point of an object not in the axis, when seen (1) distinctly and (2) indistinctly.

If the focal length of a convex lens be 3 inches, and the shortest distance of distinct vision be 6 inches, prove that, when the eye is always placed so as to see distinctly under the greatest possible angle, the lens magnifies when within 6 inches of the object, and diminishes at greater distances.

xii. Trace the course of an oblique pencil of rays from a star to the eye through the common Astronomical Telescope; and calculate the magnifying power, when the telescope is adjusted for vision by rays diverging from a given distance from the eye-glass.

If the object-glass be divided, so as to form two semicircular lenses, and these be displaced along the line of division, what must be the displacement of the centres in order that a double star may appear as three stars?

THURSDAY, *January* 5. 9 to 12.

i. THREE concentric circles are drawn in the same plane. Draw a straight line, such that one of its segments between the inner and outer circumference may be bisected at one of the points in which the line meets the middle circumference.

ii. A quadrilateral circumscribes an ellipse. Prove that either pair of opposite sides subtends supplementary angles at either focus.

iii. A polygon of a given number of sides circumscribes an ellipse. Prove that, when its area is a minimum, any side is parallel to the line joining the points of contact of the two adjacent sides.

4. If the tangent at any point P of an hyperbola cut an asymptote in T, and if SP cut the same asymptote in Q, then $SQ = QT$.

5. Prove that the sum of the products of the first n natural numbers taken two and two together is
$$\frac{(n-1)n(n+1)(3n+2)}{24}.$$

6. The centres of the escribed circles of a triangle must lie without the circumscribing circle, and cannot be equidistant from it unless the triangle be equilateral.

vii. If perpendiculars be drawn from the angles of an equilateral triangle upon any tangent to the inscribed circle, prove that the sum of the reciprocals of those perpendiculars which fall upon the same side of the tangent is equal to the reciprocal of that perpendicular which falls upon the opposite side.

viii. Four equal particles are mutually repulsive, the law of force being that of the inverse distance. If they be joined together by four inextensible strings of given length so as to form a quadrilateral, prove that, when there is equilibrium, the four particles lie in a circle.

9. A heavy rod is placed in any manner resting on two points of a rough horizontal curve, and a string attached to the middle point C of the chord is pulled in any direction so that the rod is on the point of motion. Prove that the locus of the intersection

of the string with the directions of the frictions at the points of support is an arc of a circle and a part of a straight line.

Find also how the force must be applied that its intersections with the frictions may trace out the remainder of the circle.

x. A rigid wire without appreciable mass is formed into an arc of an equiangular spiral and carries a small heavy particle fixed in its pole. If the convexity of the wire be placed in contact with a perfectly rough horizontal plane, prove that the point of contact with the plane will move with uniform acceleration, and find this acceleration.

11. If two parabolas be placed with their axes vertical, vertices downwards, and foci coincident, prove that there are three chords down which the time of descent of a particle under the action of gravity from one curve to the other is a minimum, and that one of these is the principal diameter and the other two make an angle of $60°$ with it on either side.

12. If a particle slide along a chord of a circle under the action of a centre of force varying as the distance, the time will be the same for all chords provided they terminate at either extremity of the diameter through the centre of force.

13. A hollow cone floats with its vertex downwards in a cylindrical vessel containing water. Determine the equal quantities of water that may be poured into the cone and into the cylinder that the position of the cone in space may be unaltered.

xiv. A hemispherical bowl is filled to the brim with fluid, and a rod specifically heavier than the fluid rests with one end in contact with the concave surface of the bowl and passes over the rim of the bowl, find an equation for determining the position of equilibrium.

xv. A ray of light passes through a medium of which the refractive index at any point is inversely proportional to the distance of that point from a certain plane. Prove that the path of the ray is a circular arc of which the centre is in the above-mentioned plane.

16. A small bead is projected with any velocity along a circular wire under the action of a force varying inversely as the fifth power of the distance from a centre of force situated in the circumference. Prove that the pressure on the wire is constant.

17. A bright spot of white light is viewed through a right

cone of glass the vertex of which is pointed directly towards the spot. Describe the appearances seen; and prove that, if a section of the locus of the images corresponding to different values of the refractive index be made by a plane through the axis of the cone, it will be a rectangular hyperbola.

xviii. An elastic string passes through a smooth straight tube whose length is the natural length of the string. It is then pulled out equally at both ends until its length is increased by $\sqrt{2}$ times its original length. Two equal perfectly elastic balls are attached to the extremities and projected with equal velocities at right angles to the string and so as to impinge upon each other. Prove that the time of impact is independent of the velocity of projection, and that after impact each ball will move in a straight line, assuming that the tension of the string is proportional to the extension throughout the motion.

xix. A particle is projected along a chord of an ellipse from any point in the curve, and when it again meets the ellipse has a certain impulse towards the centre of the ellipse impressed upon it, causing it again to describe a chord, and so on for any number of times. Prove that, if after a given number of such impulses, the particle pass through another given point on the circumference of the curve, the polygonal area so described about the centre is a maximum, when the successive chords are described in equal times.

THURSDAY, *January* 5. 1 to 4.

1. ENUNCIATE and prove Newton's second Lemma.

Hence prove that two quantities may vanish in an infinite ratio to one another; and explain accurately what is meant by this phrase.

2. Enunciate and prove Newton's tenth Lemma.

If the curve employed in the proof of this lemma be an arc of a parabola, the axis of which is perpendicular to the straight line on which time is measured, prove that the accelerating effect of the force will vary as the distance from the axis of the parabola.

3. If particles describe different circles with uniform velocity, their accelerations tend to the centres of the circles; and are to each other as the squares of arcs described in the same time, divided by the radii of the circles.

One circle rolls uniformly within another of twice its radius; prove that the resultant acceleration of a particle situated on the circumference of the rolling circle tends to the centre of the fixed circle, and varies as the distance from that centre.

iv. Prove that the accelerating effect of a force, under the action of which a body moves in a central orbit, is measured by the ultimate value of $2\dfrac{QR}{T^2}$, QR being the subtense, parallel to the direction of the force at P, of the arc PQ described in the time T.

Deduce the equation $V^2 = \tfrac{1}{2}F \cdot PV$.

Prove that, when a body moves along a smooth tube under the action of any force tending to a point and varying as the distance from the point, the difference of the squares of the velocities at the beginning and end of an arc varies as the difference of the squares of the distances of the extremities of the arc from the fixed point.

v. Find the law of force tending to the centre of an ellipse, under the action of which a body can describe the ellipse.

A body is revolving in an ellipse under the action of such a force, and when it arrives at the extremity of the major axis, the force ceases to act until the body has moved through a distance equal to the semi-minor axis, it then acts for a quarter of the periodic time in the ellipse; prove that, if it again ceases to act for the same time as before, the body will have arrived at the other extremity of the major axis.

vi. When a body revolves in an ellipse under the action of a force tending to the focus, find the velocity at any point of its orbit, and the periodic time.

If on arriving at the extremity of the minor axis, the force has its law changed, so that it varies as the distance, the magnitude at that point remaining the same, the periodic time will be unaltered, and the sum of the new axes is to their difference as the sum of the old axes to the distance between the foci.

vii. Explain the changes in the length of days in the north temperate zone, during the passage of the Earth from Libra to Aries.

Describe the position of the Earth in its orbit to-day, and our position on it at three o'clock this afternoon with reference to the ecliptic and the position of the Sun.

viii. Describe the apparent path of the Moon with reference to the Earth and the Sun, shewing by a figure the direction of the curvature of its absolute path; and shew how many Lunar Eclipses can occur in a year.

What distance of the Moon would, with the same inclination of the orbit, have ensured an eclipse at every opposition?

ix. Explain the use of the reading microscope in the mural circle; and prove that, when a pair of microscopes is used, the error arising from want of perfect coincidence in the centres of rotation and graduation, will be eliminated if the axes of the microscopes be coincident.

Shew how a double observation is made with the mural circle.

10. Explain the origin of the tides; and prove that, supposing the Earth to be accurately a sphere covered with water, when it is high water at a given point on the surface of the globe, it is also high water at the antipodes of that point. Prove that the highest spring tides will take place at the time of an eclipse.

11. Define a tropical, a sidereal, and an anomalistic year; stating to which of the three the average length of a civil year is adjusted, and why.

Explain the statement, that the perihelion of the Earth's orbit completes a tropical revolution in about 20,000 years, and a sidereal revolution in about 100,000.

12. Define Parallax; stating how the position of a heavenly body is affected by it. In what positions of a star are its right ascension and declination respectively unaffected by it? State also which of the heavenly bodies is most affected by it, and in what position it is so.

Monday, *January* 16. 9 to 12.

1. Investigate the conditions necessary and sufficient for the equilibrium of a rigid body, acted on by any number of forces in any directions in space.

A uniform heavy ellipsoid has a given point in contact with a smooth horizontal plane. Find the plane of the couple necessary to keep it at rest in this position; and investigate its equation referred to the principal axes of the ellipsoid.

2. If a heavy rigid body rest upon more than three immoveable points of support, prove that the pressure at each point is indeterminate.

An oblong table has the legs at the four corners alike in all respects and slightly compressible. Supposing the floor and top of the table to be perfectly rigid, find the pressures on the legs, when the table is loaded in any given manner, supposing the compression to be proportional to the pressure; and prove that, when the resultant weight lies in one of four straight lines on the surface of the table, the table is supported by three legs only.

3. Find the equations of equilibrium of a perfectly flexible uniform inextensible string when acted on by any given forces.

If a small rough heavy bead be strung upon such a string, and the string be suspended from two points and acted on by gravity only, write down the equations for determining within what portion of the string it is possible for the bead to rest.

iv. Prove that, when any number of particles $P_1, P_2, ... P_n$ are moving in any manner, the acceleration of P_n is the resultant of the accelerations of P_n relative to P_{n-1}, of P_{n-1} relative to P_{n-2}, ... of P_2 relative to P_1, and of P_1.

A particle is attached by a rod without mass, to the extremity of another rod, n times as long, which revolves in a given manner about the other extremity, the whole motion taking place in a horizontal plane. If θ be the inclination of the rods, ω the angular velocity of the second rod at the time t, prove that

$$\frac{d^2\theta}{dt^2} + \frac{d\omega}{dt} + n\left(\frac{d\omega}{dt}\cos\theta + \omega^2\sin\theta\right) = 0.$$

v. A bead is capable of free motion on a fine smooth wire in the form of any plane curve, and is acted on by given forces; compare the pressure on the wire with the weight of the bead.

If the wire be a horizontal circle, radius a, and the bead be acted on only by the tension of an elastic string, the natural length of which is a, fixed to a point in the plane of the circle at distance $2a$ from its centre, find the condition that the bead may just revolve; and prove that in this case the pressures at the extremities of the diameter through the fixed point will be twice and four times the weight of the bead if that weight be such as to stretch the string to double its natural length.

vi. Find the nature of the orbit, when a particle moves under the action of a central force which varies inversely as the cube of the distance.

If a particle, acted on by a central force, and moving in a resisting medium in which the retardation $= \kappa$ (vel.)^2 describe an equiangular spiral, the pole of which is the centre of force; prove that the central force

$$\propto \frac{1}{r^3} e^{-\frac{2\kappa r}{\cos a}},$$

where a is the angle of the spiral.

vii. If an incompressible fluid be in equilibrium under the action of any forces, prove that the direction of the resultant force at any point is perpendicular to the surface of equal pressure at that point.

If the particles of a mass of fluid rotating uniformly about a fixed axis, attract one another according to such a law that the surfaces of equal pressure are similar coaxial oblate spheroids, prove that the resultant attraction of a spheroid, the particles of which attract according to the same law, is the resultant of two forces perpendicular to the equator and the axis of revolution respectively, and varying as the distance of the attracted point from them.

viii. Prove that, when the density of a mass of air is suddenly changed from ρ to ρ', the pressure is altered in the ratio $\left(\frac{\rho'}{\rho}\right)^K$, where K is the ratio of the specific heats of air, on the suppositions of the pressure and volume remaining constant respectively.

9. A small pencil of light, diverging from a given point, passes centrically and with small obliquity through a lens; determine the position of the primary focal line.

A distant circular window is viewed by a short-sighted man through his eye-glass, the axis of which passes through the centre of the window and is perpendicular to its plane. Prove that the image of the window formed by primary focal lines will be spherical, provided the window be filled with concentric rings of stained glass, and the refractive index of the colour throughout any ring be

$$\mu - \frac{(\mu-1)(2\mu+1)}{2\mu} \cdot \frac{r^2}{d^2},$$

μ being the index of the central colour, r the radius of the ring in question, and d the distance of the window from the lens.

x. Prove that, in order to determine the time at a given place by a single altitude of a star, the most favourable stars to observe are those near the prime vertical.

11. Find the parallax in right ascension of a heavenly body, in terms of the latitude of the place of observation, and the hour angle and declination of the body, assuming the distance of the body from the Earth to be so great that the sine and circular measure of the parallax may be considered equal.

Shew that the locus of all the bodies, which on this assumption have their parallaxes in right ascension for a given place and time equal to a given quantity, is a right circular cylinder touching the plane of the meridian of the place along the axis of the heavens.

MONDAY, *January* 16. 1½ to 4.

1. SHEW how to expand a^x in a series of ascending powers of x.

Prove that the series

$$1 + \frac{2^3}{1.2} + \frac{3^3}{1.2.3} + \frac{4^3}{1.2.3.4} + \ldots = 5e.$$

ii. Prove de Moivre's theorem; and thence prove that, whatever be the unit of angular measure, if $\cos 1 + \sqrt{(-1)} \sin 1 = k$,

$$\cos\theta = \frac{k^\theta + k^{-\theta}}{2}, \quad \sin\theta = \frac{k^\theta - k^{-\theta}}{2\sqrt{(-1)}}.$$

Prove also that the limit of $\dfrac{\sin\theta}{\theta}$, as θ is indefinitely diminished, is

$$\frac{\log_e k}{\sqrt{(-1)}}.$$

iii. Give Cardan's solution of a cubic equation: and prove that, when the roots are all real, they will be exhibited under an imaginary form.

Solve the equation, $x^3 - 6x - 9 = 0$.

iv. Enunciate Sturm's Theorem; and apply it to find the number and position of the real roots of the equation,

$$x^3 + 6x^2 + 4 = 0.$$

v. Find the area of the triangle, the co-ordinates of the angular points of which are (h_1, k_1), (h_2, k_2), (h_3, k_3).

Hence deduce the equation of a straight line passing through two given points.

vi. Find the value of p, in order that the straight line represented by the equation, $x \cos \theta + y \sin \theta = p$, may touch the ellipse

$$\frac{x^2}{a^2} + \frac{y^2}{b^2} = 1.$$

Prove that the locus of the vertices of an equilateral triangle described about the ellipse, $\frac{x^2}{a^2} + \frac{y^2}{b^2} = 1$, is given by the equation

$$4(b^2x^2 + a^2y^2 - a^2b^2) = 3(x^2 + y^2 - a^2 - b^2)^2.$$

vii. Investigate the criterion by which it is determined whether the equation, $ax^2 + 2bxy + cy^2 + 2dx + 2ey + 1 = 0$, represents an ellipse, parabola, or hyperbola.

Prove that, however rectangular co-ordinate axes be shifted, the ratio of the quantities $b^2 - ac$, $(a+c)^2$, will remain unaltered. What is the geometrical meaning of this ratio?

8. Investigate the condition that the straight lines

$$\frac{x-a}{l} = \frac{y-b}{m} = \frac{z-c}{n},$$

$$\frac{x-a'}{l'} = \frac{y-b'}{m'} = \frac{z-c'}{n'},$$

may be at right angles to one another.

Prove that, if a straight line be drawn from the origin to cut the first of the above straight lines at right angles, its equations will be

$$\frac{x}{a-lt} = \frac{y}{b-mt} = \frac{z}{c-nt},$$

where $t = \dfrac{al + bm + cn}{l^2 + m^2 + n^2}.$

9. Find the equation of a plane in the form

$$lx + my + nz - p = 0,$$

where l, m, n, are its direction-cosines.

If a, β, γ be the distances of a point from the three faces of a tetrahedron which meet in the vertex, prove that the equation of the plane passing through the vertex, and through the centres of the circles inscribed in and circumscribed about the base, is

$$(\cos B - \cos C) p_1 a + (\cos C - \cos A) p_2 \beta + (\cos A - \cos B) p_3 \gamma = 0,$$

where A, B, C are the angles of the base, and p_1, p_2, p_3 the perpendiculars from the vertex on the sides of the base.

10. Define the polar plane of a given point with respect to a given sphere; and find its equation, referred to the centre of the sphere as origin.

Find the equation of the sphere, passing through a given point and through the circle in which the polar plane of that point with respect to a given sphere cuts that sphere.

11. Shew how to find the real circular sections of the surface of which the equation is

$$Ax^2 + By^2 + Cz^2 = 1;$$

and describe their positions relative to the different classes of surfaces represented by the above equation.

If a sphere touch an ellipsoid and also cut it, the common section cannot be a plane curve unless the point of contact be one of four fixed points on the ellipsoid.

TUESDAY, *January* 17. 9 to 12.

i. FIND a point the distances of which from three given points, not in the same straight line, are proportional to p, q and r respectively, the four points being in the same plane.

2. If TP, TQ be two tangents drawn from any point T to touch a conic in P and Q, and if S and H be the foci, then

$$\frac{ST^2}{SP.SQ} = \frac{HT^2}{HP.HQ}.$$

iii. A polygon is inscribed in an ellipse so that each side subtends the same angle at one of the foci. Prove that, if the alternate sides be produced to meet, their points of intersection will lie on a conic section having the same focus and directrix as the original ellipse, and that the chords joining the consecutive points of intersection all subtend the same constant angle at the focus as the sides of the original polygon.

4. Prove that the equiangular spiral is the only curve such that its radius of curvature is proportional to the reciprocal of the radius of curvature at the corresponding point of the reciprocal polar.

5. If two plane sections of a right cone be taken, having the same directrix, the foci corresponding to that directrix lie on a straight line which passes through the vertex.

vi. Find the equation of the envelope of the perpendiculars to the successive focal radii of a parabola drawn through the extremities of these radii.

vii. If two concentric rectangular hyperbolas have a common tangent, the lines joining their points of intersection to their respective points of contact with the common tangent will subtend equal angles at their common centre.

viii. If P be a point on a geodesic line AP, drawn on a conoidal surface, s the length of AP, σ, N, and O the projections of s, P, and the axis on any plane perpendicular to the axis, and p the projection of ON on the tangent to AP at P, then

$$\frac{dp}{d\sigma} = \frac{d\sigma}{ds}.$$

9. A string is placed on a smooth plane curve under the action of a central force F, tending to a point in the same plane; prove that, if the curve be such that a particle could freely describe it under the action of that force, the pressure of the string on the curve referred to a unit of length will be $= \dfrac{F \sin \phi}{2} + \dfrac{c}{\rho}$, where ϕ is the angle which the radius vector from the centre of force makes with the tangent, ρ is the radius of curvature, and c is an arbitrary constant.

If the curve be an equiangular spiral with the centre of force in the pole, and if one end of the string rest freely on the spiral at a distance a from the pole, then the pressure is equal to

$$\frac{\mu \sin \phi}{2r} \left(\frac{1}{r^2} + \frac{1}{a^2} \right).$$

10. If a string, the particles of which repel each other with a force varying as the distance, be in equilibrium when fastened to two fixed points, prove that the tension at any point varies as the square root of the radius of curvature.

11. If any uniform arc of an equiangular spiral attract a particle, placed at the pole with a force varying inversely as the square of the distance, prove that the resultant attraction acts along the line joining the pole with the intersection of the tangents at the extremities of the arc.

Prove also that, if any other given curve possess this same property, the law of attraction must be $F = \dfrac{\mu}{p^3} \dfrac{dp}{dr}$, where p is the perpendicular drawn from the attracted particle on the tangent at the point of which the radius vector is r.

xii. A material particle is acted on by a force the direction of which always meets an infinite straight line AB at right angles, and the intensity of which is inversely proportional to the cube of the distance of the particle from the line. The particle is projected with the velocity from infinity from a point P at a distance a from the nearest point O of the line in a direction perpendicular to OP, and inclined at the angle α to the plane AOP. Prove that the particle is always on the sphere of which O is the centre, that it meets every meridian line through AB at the angle α, and that it reaches the line AB in the time

$$\frac{a^2}{\sqrt{(\mu)} \cos \alpha},$$

μ being the absolute force.

13. If a particle slide along a smooth curve which turns with uniform angular velocity ω about a fixed point O, then the velocity of the particle relatively to the moving curve is given by the equation

$$v^2 = c^2 + \omega^2 r^2,$$

where r is the distance of the particle from the point O; and the pressure on the curve will be given by the formula

$$\frac{R}{m} = \frac{v^2}{\rho} + \omega^2 p + 2\omega v,$$

where m is the mass of the particle, and p the perpendicular from O on the tangent.

14. A string is laid on a smooth table in the form of a catenary, and an impulse is communicated to one extremity in the direction of the tangent, prove (1) that the initial velocity of any point, resolved parallel to the directrix, is proportional to the inverse square of the distance of that point from the directrix, and

(2) that the velocity of the centre of gravity of any arc, resolved in the same direction, is proportional to the angle between the tangents at extremities of the arc directly, and to the length of the arc inversely.

xv. A right circular cone floats with its axis horizontal in a fluid, the specific gravity of which is double that of the cone, the vertex of the cone being attached to a fixed point in the surface of the fluid. Prove that for stability of equilibrium the semi-vertical angle of the cone must be less than $60°$.

xvi. A ribbon of very small uniform thickness h is coiled up tightly into a cylindrical form, and placed with its curved surface in contact with a perfectly rough plane inclined to the horizon at an angle a, the axis of the cylinder being parallel to the intersection of the plane with the horizon. Prove that the time in which the whole will be unrolled is very approximately

$$\frac{\pi}{4}\sqrt{\left(\frac{Gd^2}{gh\sin a}\right)},$$

where d is the diameter of the original coil.

17. If three beads, the masses of which are m, m', m'', slide along the sides of a smooth triangle ABC, and attract each other with forces which vary as the distance, find the position of equilibrium. Prove also that, if they be slightly disturbed, the displacement of each will be given by a series of three terms of the form

$$L\sin(nt + \lambda),$$

where L and λ are arbitrary constants, and the values of n are the three positive roots of the equation

$$(n^2 - a)(n^2 - \beta)(n^2 - \gamma) - \cos^2 A\, m'm''(n^2 - a) - \cos^2 B\, m''m(n^2 - \beta)$$
$$- \cos^2 C\, mm'(n^2 - \gamma) - 2\cos A\cos B\cos C\, mm'm'' = 0,$$

where a, β, γ represent $m'' + m'$, $m + m''$, $m' + m$ respectively.

xviii. The bore of a gun barrel is formed by the motion of an ellipse of which the centre is in the axis of the barrel, and the plane is perpendicular to that axis, the centre moving along the axis, and the ellipse revolving in its own plane with an angular velocity always bearing the same ratio to the linear velocity of its centre. A spheroidal ball fitting the barrel is fired from the gun.

If v be the velocity with which the ball would have emerged from the barrel had there been no twist; prove that the velocity of rotation with which it actually emerges in the case supposed is

$$\frac{2\pi n v}{\sqrt{(l^2 + 4\pi^2 n^2 k^2)}},$$

the number of revolutions of the ellipse corresponding to the whole length l of the barrel being n, and k being the radius of gyration of the ball about the axis coinciding with the axis of the barrel, and the gun being supposed to be immovable.

XIX. An elastic ring of length l, mass m, and elasticity E is placed over the vertex of a smooth cone, the semi-vertical angle of which is a, and stretched upon it to any size. Supposing it then set free, prove that the time before it leaves the cone is

$$\frac{1}{4}\sqrt{\left(\frac{ml}{E}\right)} \operatorname{cosec} a,$$

the action of gravity being neglected.

TUESDAY, *Jan.* 17. 1½ to 4.

1. INVESTIGATE the condition of achromatism which is required in Huyghens' eye-piece; and find the magnifying power of Gregory's Telescope with this eye-piece. Draw a figure representing the course of the pencil.

2. If pq be the image of PQ, placed perpendicular to the axis QCq of a lens or mirror CR, QRq the course of a ray from Q to q, shew that $PQ : pq :: RqC : RQC$.

Hence prove that, with all combinations of lenses for eye-pieces, the magnifying power of a telescope, arranged for parallel or diverging emergent pencils, is the ratio of the diameter of the object-glass or mirror to that of its image formed on emergence from the eye-piece.

iii. Define the equation of time; state the causes to which it is due, and prove that it vanishes four times a year. Find also roughly when it attains its maxima and minima values, assuming the longitude of perihelion to be $100°$.

iv. Two particles move under the influence of gravity, and of their mutual attractions; prove that their centre of gravity will describe a parabola, and that each particle will describe, relatively to that point, areas proportional to the times.

5. Define a principal axis through any point of a rigid body; and, having given one principal axis through a point, find the positions of the other two.

Prove that the locus of a point, through which one of the principal axes is in a given direction, is a rectangular hyperbola in the plane of which the centre of gravity lies, and of which one of the asymptotes is in the given direction; unless the given direction be that of one of the principal axes through the centre of gravity.

vi. Investigate the effect of the central disturbing force on the position of the apsides of the Moon's orbit, supposing the line of apsides near syzygy.

By what two causes is the excess of progression over regression, during a synodic revolution of the Sun and line of apsides increased?

vii. If p be the pressure, and ρ the density, at any point, x, y, z of a mass of fluid in motion, u, v, w the component velocities of the fluid at that point, X, Y, Z the component accelerations due to the forces acting on the fluid parallel to the co-ordinate axes, investigate the equations.

$$\frac{1}{\rho}\frac{dp}{dx} = X - \frac{du}{dt} - u\frac{du}{dx} - v\frac{du}{dy} - w\frac{du}{dz},$$

$$\frac{1}{\rho}\frac{dp}{dy} = Y - \frac{dv}{dt} - u\frac{dv}{dx} - v\frac{dv}{dy} - w\frac{dv}{dz},$$

$$\frac{1}{\rho}\frac{dp}{dz} = Z - \frac{dw}{dt} - u\frac{dw}{dx} - v\frac{dw}{dy} - w\frac{dw}{dz}.$$

State the hypothesis of steady motion; and point out the modification which will be introduced into the above equations, if the motion be steady.

8. Give a full account of the methods of approximation adopted in the Lunar Theory; and state of what circumstances advantage is taken in order to conduct the approximation to the solution of the equations in the Planetary Theory.

9. Assuming the equations

$$\frac{d^2u}{d\theta^2} + u + 2\left(\frac{d^2u}{d\theta^2} + u\right)\int \frac{Td\theta}{h^2u^3} + \frac{T}{h^2u^3}\frac{du}{d\theta} - \frac{P}{h^2u^2} = 0,$$

$$P = \mu u^2\left(1 - \frac{3a}{2}s^2\right) - \frac{m'u'^3}{2u}\{1 + 3\cos 2(\theta - \theta')\},$$

$$T = -\frac{3m'u'^3}{2u}\sin 2(\theta - \theta'),$$

investigate that term in u the argument of which is

$$(2 - 2m - 2c)\theta - 2\beta + 2a.$$

WEDNESDAY, *Jan.* 18. 9 to 12.

1. A PARABOLA touches one side of a triangle in its middle point and the other two sides produced. Prove that the perpendiculars drawn from the angles of the triangle upon any tangent to the parabola are in harmonical progression.

2. Find the length of the longest straight line which can be drawn in the interval between two similar similarly situated and concentric ellipsoids; and, if a line shorter than the line so determined be moved about in the interval, prove that its point of contact with the interior ellipsoid can never lie within the cone represented by the equation

$$\frac{x^2}{a^2\{a^2(1-m^2)-r^2\}} + \frac{y^2}{b^2\{b^2(1-m^2)-r^2\}} + \frac{z^2}{c^2\{c^2(1-m^2)-r^2\}} = 0,$$

a, b, c being the semi-axes of the outer ellipsoid, m the ratio of the linear magnitudes of the inner and outer ellipsoid, and $2r$ the length of the line in question, which is assumed greater than

$$2b\sqrt{(1-m^2)}.$$

What is the meaning of the boundary so determined when $2r$ is less than $2b\sqrt{(1-m^2)}$ and greater than $2c\sqrt{(1-m^2)}$?

3. If, in a rigid body moving in any manner about a fixed point, a series of points be taken along any straight line in the body, and through these points straight lines be drawn in the direction of the instantaneous motion of the points, prove that the locus of these straight lines is an hyperbolic paraboloid.

4. If $f(x, y, z) = 0$ be the equation to a surface, and r be a straight line drawn through the point x, y, z of which the magnitude and direction are any given functions of x, y, z, state what is the relation between the original surface and that whose equation is $n^{r\frac{d}{dr}} f(x, y, z) = 0$, supposing that in the latter equation x, y, and z have been expressed in terms of r and any two other variables independent of r, and that n is a given numerical quantity, and prove that if the two surfaces coincide for all values of n, the line r must lie altogether in either of them.

Apply this to find the partial differential equations of conical and conoidal surfaces respectively when referred to any system of rectangular axes.

5. From a flexible envelope in the form of an oblate spheroid, of which the eccentricity of the generating ellipse is e, the part between two meridians, the planes of which are inclined to each other at the angle $2\pi(1 - e)$, is cut away and the edges are then sewed together; prove that the meridian curve of the new envelope will be the curve of sines.

6. If an uniform inextensible and flexible string be stretched over a smooth surface of revolution, prove that the following equations hold:

$$\frac{d}{ds}\left(Tr\frac{dx}{ds}\right) + Xr = 0,$$

$$\frac{d}{ds}\left(Tr\frac{dy}{ds}\right) - T\frac{dr}{dy} + Yr = 0,$$

where ds is the element of the string at any point, dx and dy are corresponding elements of the arc of the circle through that point perpendicular to the meridian, and of the meridian respectively, X and Y are the resolved parts of the impressed forces along these directions, and r is the distance from the axis, the mass of an unit of length of the string being taken as unity. Hence prove that, if such a string be acted upon by a force at all points perpendicular to the axis of revolution, and inversely proportional to the square of the distance from that axis, the string will, if properly suspended, cut every meridian in the same angle.

7. A string is wound round a vertical cylinder of radius a in the form of a given helix, the inclination to the horizon being i. The upper end is attached to a fixed point in the cylinder, and the lower, a portion of the string of length $l \sec i$ having been unwound, has a material particle attached to it which is also

in contact with a rough horizontal plane, the coefficient of friction being μ. Supposing a horizontal velocity V perpendicular to the free portion of the string to be applied to the particle so as to tend to wind the string on the cylinder, determine the motion; and prove that the particle will leave the plane after the projection of the unwound portion of string upon the plane has described the angle of which the circular measure is

$$\frac{1}{2\mu \tan i} \cdot \log \frac{ag}{2\mu \tan^2 i \cdot V^2 - 2\mu g l \tan i + ag}.$$

8. A particle is acted on by two centres of force residing in the same point, one attractive, the other repulsive, and varying inversely as the square and cube of the distance respectively. Two consecutive equal apsidal distances are drawn and the portion of the plane of motion included between them is rolled into a right circular cone. Prove that the trajectory described under the circumstances mentioned above becomes a plane curve on the surface of the cone, and that it will be an ellipse, parabola, or hyperbola, according as the velocity in the trajectory was less than, equal to, or greater than that from infinity.

9. A particle is describing an orbit round a centre of force which is any function of the distance, and is acted upon by a disturbing force which is always perpendicular to the plane of the instantaneous orbit and inversely proportional to the distance of the body from the original centre of force. Prove that the plane of the instantaneous orbit revolves uniformly round its instantaneous axis.

10. A die in the form of a parallelopiped the edges of which are $2a$, $2b$, and $2c$, is loaded in such a manner that the centre of gravity remains coincident with the centre of figure, but the principal moments of inertia about the centre of gravity become equal; if it then fall from any height and without rotation upon a horizontal plane composed of adhesive material so that no point which has once come in contact with the plane can separate from it, prove that the chance of one of the faces bounded by the edges $2b$, $2c$ coming uppermost is

$$\frac{2}{\pi} \sin^{-1} \frac{bc}{\sqrt{\{(a^2 + b^2)(a^2 + c^2)\}}}.$$

11. A uniform sphere is placed in contact with the exterior surface of a perfectly rough cone. Its centre is acted on by a force,

the direction of which always meets the axis of the cone at right angles, and the intensity of which varies inversely as the cube of the distance from that axis. Prove that, if the sphere be properly started, the path described by its centre will meet every generating line of the cone on which it lies in the same angle.

12. A small rigid vertical cylinder, containing air, is rigidly closed at the bottom, and covered at the top by a disk of very small weight which fits it air-tight. Supposing the air in the cylinder to be set in vibration, prove that the period of a vibration is $\dfrac{2\pi}{m}$, m being a root of the equation

$$m \tan \frac{ml}{a} = \frac{\kappa \beta \Pi}{\mu a};$$

where l is the length of the tube, a the velocity of sound in air, μ the mass, κ the area of the disk, $p \propto \rho(1+\beta s)$ the relation between the pressure and density when the latter is suddenly changed from ρ to $\rho(1+s)$, and Π the pressure of the air in the cylinder before motion commences.

13. A circular drumhead of uniform thickness is stretched with a tension of uniform magnitude at all points in its circumference, and is then set in vibration by a small disturbance commencing at the centre. Prove (1) that if z be the transversal disturbance at the time t of a point the initial distance of which from the centre was r, then

$$\frac{d^2z}{dt^2} = a^2 \left(\frac{1}{r}\frac{dz}{dr} + \frac{d^2z}{dr^2} \right),$$

and (2) that the general primitive of this differential equation is

$$z = \int_0^\pi \phi(at + r\cos\theta)\, d\theta + \int_0^\pi \psi(at + r\cos\theta)\log(r\sin^2\theta)\, d\theta,$$

ϕ and ψ being arbitrary functions, and a a constant depending upon the tension and constitution of the drumhead.

WEDNESDAY, *Jan.* 18. 1½ to 4.

1. DEFINE the terms Limit, Independent and Dependent Variable, and Differential Coefficient.

If x represent the time which has elapsed since a given epoch, and y the space which a moving point has described in that time, what will $\dfrac{dy}{dx}$ represent?

ii. Prove that $\dfrac{f(x)}{\phi(x)} = \dfrac{f'(\theta x)}{\phi'(\theta x)}$, where θ lies between 0 and 1, with certain limitations: and deduce Stirling's Theorem.

3. Change the independent variables in

$$x\frac{d^2V}{dx^2} + y\frac{d^2V}{dy^2} + \tfrac{1}{2}\left(\frac{dV}{dx} + \frac{dV}{dy}\right),$$

from x and y to u and v, having given $x + y = u$, $y = uv$.

4. Explain the use of the method of indeterminate multipliers in determining the values of a function of several variables connected by given equations, which are maxima or minima.

Find the position of the point, the sum of the squares on the distances of which from the three sides of a triangle is the least possible; and prove that the angles, which the sides respectively subtend at this point, exceed the supplements of those which they subtend at the centre of gravity of the triangle by the respective angles of the triangle.

v. Prove that, if a curve represented by an algebraical equation have an asymptote, and the curve lies on the same side at both ends, there will be an odd number of points at an infinite distance in which the asymptote meets the curve.

vi. Trace the curves represented by the equations

$$(x^2 - 4a^2)y^2 - 12a^2x(a-y) = 0 \quad\ldots\ldots\ldots\ldots(1),$$
$$\sin y - m \sin x = 0 \quad\ldots\ldots\ldots\ldots(2).$$

In (1) explain the circumstance that the asymptotes parallel to the axis of y appear to contradict the statement of (v.). In (2) distinguish between the cases in which $m > =$ or < 1.

vii. If $f(x, y) = 0$ be the equation of a curve in a rational integral form, in which (x_0, y_0) is a multiple point through which n branches pass; shew that the directions of the branches are determined by the equation

$$\phi^{(n)}(0) = 0, \text{ where } \phi(r) = f(x_0 + lr, y_0 + mr).$$

Find the form of the curve represented by the equation

$$(y - b)^n - (x^2 - 2ax)^3 - a^6 = 0,$$

at the multiple point.

viii. Find the co-ordinates of the centre of curvature at any point of a plane curve.

The equation of a circle is $x^2 + y^2 = c^2$, prove that the equation of the directrix of a parabola of which the axis is parallel to the axis of x and which has the closest possible contact at the point (x_0, y_0) is $2x = 3x_0$.

9. Integrate the following differentials:

$$\frac{dx}{x^2(h+x)^{\frac{1}{2}}}, \quad \frac{d\theta}{(m+n\cos\theta)^2}, \quad \frac{dx}{(x^2 - 2ax + a^2 + c^2)(x-b)^2},$$

and evaluate $\int_0^{\frac{\pi}{2}} \log \sin \theta \, d\theta$.

10. Prove that the area of a curve, represented by the equation $f(x, y) = 0$, will be given by the formula $\frac{1}{2}\int(xdy - ydx)$, the integrals being taken within proper limits.

One circle rolls within another; apply the above formula to find the area of the curve traced out by a given point within the rolling circle.

xi. Prove that, if a plane intersect a surface, it will generally be a tangent plane to the surface at every multiple point of the curve of intersection. What exceptions are there?

Prove that a tangent plane to a developable surface meets the surface in a straight line and a curve touching that straight line.

xii. Explain generally the principle of Variation of Parameters, as applied to the solution of a differential equation; and illustrate this method of solution by assuming the result in the form of that obtained from the first three terms f

$$\frac{d^2y}{dx^2} - 2m\frac{dy}{dx} + m^2 y + \frac{1}{2x}\left(\frac{dy}{dx} - my\right) = 0.$$

13. Define a developable surface; and, from your definition, deduce the partial differential equation of such surfaces.

Find the equation of the developable surface generated by the plane which moves in such a manner as to be always in contact with the surfaces

$$\frac{x^2}{a^2} + \frac{y^2}{b^2} + \frac{z^2}{c^2} = 1,$$

$$\frac{x^2}{a^2 - r^2} + \frac{y^2}{b^2 - r^2} + \frac{z^2}{c^2 - r^2} = 1.$$

14. Explain what is meant by $\Delta^n.0^m$; and prove that, if $f(e^t)$ be expanded in a series proceeding by ascending powers of t, the coefficient of t^m is $\dfrac{f(1 + \Delta) 0^m}{1.2\ldots\ldots m}$.

Prove that, if m be less than r,

$$\{1 + \log(1 + \Delta)\}^r.\,0^m = r(r-1)(r-2)\ldots(r-m+1).$$

THURSDAY, *Jan.* 19. 9 to 12.

1. If at the extremities P, Q of any two diameters CP, CQ of an ellipse, two tangents Pp, Qq be drawn cutting each other in T and the diameters produced in p and q, then the areas of the triangles TQp, TPq are equal.

2. If a straight line CN be drawn from the centre to bisect that chord of the circle of curvature at any point P of an ellipse which is common to the ellipse and circle, and if it be produced to cut the ellipse in Q and the tangent in T, prove that $CP = CQ$, and that each is a mean proportional between CN and CT.

3. If a, b, c be the sides of a triangle, and r the radius of the inscribed circle, then the distances of the radical centre of

the three escribed circles from the sides of the triangle will be respectively

$$r\frac{b+c}{2a}, \quad r\frac{c+a}{2b}, \quad r\frac{a+b}{2c}.$$

4. Two equal heavy particles are connected by a string which passes through a small smooth fixed ring. Prove that the equation to the plane vertical curve on which the particles will rest in all positions is,

$$r\cos\theta = a + \psi(r) - \psi(l-r),$$

where θ is the angle the radius vector makes with the vertical, l is the length of the string, ψ an arbitrary function and a an arbitrary constant.

5. If four equal particles, attracting each other with forces which vary as the distance, slide along the arc of a smooth ellipse, they cannot generally be in equilibrium unless placed at the extremities of the axes; but if a fifth equal particle be fixed at any point and attract the other four according to the same law, there will be equilibrium if the distances of the four particles from the semi-axis major be the roots of the equation

$$(y^2 - b^2)\left(y + \frac{b^2 q}{5a^2 - 3b^2}\right)^2 = -\frac{a^2 b^2 p^2}{(3a^2 - 5b^2)^2} y^2,$$

where p and q are the distances of the fifth particle from the axis minor and axis major respectively.

6. A heavy string is placed in equilibrium on a smooth sphere; prove that, if θ be the length of the spherical arc drawn from the highest point of the sphere perpendicular to the great circle touching the string at any point P, then

$$\sin\theta = \frac{a}{z+b},$$

where z is the perpendicular from P on any horizontal plane, and a, b are constants.

Shew that the form of the string can be a circle only when its plane is vertical or horizontal.

7. If three particles of masses m, m', m'', attracting each other start from rest, shew that if at any instant parallels to their directions of motion be drawn so as to form a triangle the momenta of the several particles are proportional to the sides of that triangle.

8. If from any point on a surface a number of geodesic lines be drawn in all directions, shew, (1) that those which have the greatest and least curvature of torsion bisect the angles between the principal sections, and (2) that the radius of torsion of any line, making an angle θ with a principal section, is given by the equation

$$\frac{1}{R} = \left(\frac{1}{\rho_1} - \frac{1}{\rho_2}\right) \sin\theta \cos\theta,$$

where ρ_1, ρ_2 are the radii of curvature of the principal sections.

9. If du and $d\epsilon$ be the angles of torsion and contingence of any curve of double curvature, and if $\sin\phi$ be the ratio of the radius of circular curvature to the radius of spherical curvature, prove that the square of the angle of contingence of the locus of the centres of circular curvature is

$$\overline{d\phi + du}|^2 + \cos^2\phi \overline{d\epsilon}|^2.$$

10. A particle is projected with velocity V along an infinitely thin ellipsoidal shell attracting according to the law of nature; prove that, when it leaves the ellipsoid the perpendicular from the centre on the tangent plane is $\sqrt{\left(\frac{4\pi\mu R^2 P^2}{V^2}\right)}$ where R is the radius-vector parallel to the initial direction of motion, and P the perpendicular on the tangent, μ the attraction of a mass equivalent to a unit of area of the ellipsoid at a unit of distance.

11. An infinitely thin ellipsoidal shell attracting according to the law of nature is bounded by two similar and similarly situated ellipsoids. A very small piece is cut out of the shell and replaced in its original position. Shew that the force necessary to hold the piece in equilibrium is proportional to the square of the thickness of the shell.

12. A sphere of radius a is suspended from a fixed point by a string of length l and is made to rotate about a vertical axis with an angular velocity ω. Prove that, if the string make small oscillations about its mean position, the motion of the centre of gravity will be represented by a series of terms of the form

$$L \cos(\kappa t + M),$$

where the several values of κ are the roots of the equation

$$(l\kappa^2 - g)\left(\kappa^2 - \omega\kappa - \frac{5g}{2a}\right) = \frac{5}{2}g\kappa^2.$$

13. A string is in equilibrium in the form of a circle about a centre of force in the centre. If the string be now cut at any point A, prove that the tension at any point P is instantaneously changed in the ratio of $1 - \dfrac{\epsilon^{\pi-\theta} + \epsilon^{-(\pi-\theta)}}{\epsilon^\pi + \epsilon^{-\pi}} : 1$, where θ is the angle subtended at the centre by the arc AP.

14. An inelastic string is suspended from two fixed points so that it hangs in the form of a catenary of which the parameter is c. Suppose it to make small oscillations in a vertical plane, prove the equation

$$\frac{d^2\phi}{dt^2} = \frac{g}{c}\cos^3 a\left\{\frac{d^2\phi}{da^2} + 4\phi + f(t)\right\},$$

where a is the angle the tangent at any point makes with the horizon when the string is at rest, and $a + \phi$ is the value of the same angle at the time t.

Shew that there are sufficient data to determine all the arbitrary functions.

Thursday, Jan. 19. 1½ to 4.

1. Shew that the series $u_1 + u_2 + \ldots + u_n + \ldots$ will be convergent, if the fraction $\dfrac{u_{n+1}}{u_n}$ converge to a limit less than unity as n is indefinitely increased, and divergent, if, supposing all the terms to be of the same sign, this limit be equal to or greater than unity.

Find a superior limit to the numerical values of x consistent with the convergency of the series

$$x + \frac{2^2 x^2}{1.2} + \frac{3^3 x^3}{1.2.3} + \ldots + \frac{n^n . x^n}{1.2\ldots n} + \ldots$$

2. If the sides of a spherical triangle be small compared with the radius of the sphere, then each angle of the spherical triangle

exceeds by one-third of the spherical excess the corresponding angle of the plane triangle, the sides of which are of the same length as the sides of the spherical triangle.

If the sides of a right-angled plane triangle of given area be bent so as to form a spherical triangle on a given sphere of great radius, the alteration of area in the triangle is very nearly proportional to the square of the hypothenuse.

3. If α, β, γ, be the distances of a point from three given straight lines, determine the position of the conic, $\alpha\beta = k\gamma^2$; and prove that the equation of the tangent at any point may be put into the form,

$$\lambda^2\alpha - 2\lambda\mu k^{\frac{1}{2}}\gamma + \mu^2\beta = 0.$$

Two tangents OA, OB are drawn to a conic, and are cut in P and Q by a variable tangent; prove that the locus of the centres of all circles described about the triangle OPQ is an hyperbola.

iv. If u be a function of three independent variables x, y, z, which are connected by three equations with three new independent variables ξ, η, ζ, shew how to express the partial differential coefficients of u, to the first and second orders respectively, with respect to x, y, z, in terms of the corresponding partial differential coefficients with respect to ξ, η, ζ.

Apply this method to prove that, if at a certain point in a surface $r = t$ and $s = 0$ when the axes of x and y are taken parallel to a particular pair of lines, at right angles to each other, in the tangent plane at that point, then the following relations will hold at that point whatever be the direction of the co-ordinate axes provided they be rectangular, viz.

$$\frac{r}{1+p^2} = \frac{s}{pq} = \frac{t}{1+q^2};$$

where p, q, r, s, t, denote $\frac{dz}{dx}$, $\frac{dz}{dy}$, $\frac{d^2z}{dx^2}$, $\frac{d^2z}{dxdy}$, $\frac{d^2z}{dy^2}$, respectively.

v. If the differential equations of the first order

$$\phi\left(x, y, \frac{dy}{dx}\right) = a, \quad \psi\left(x, y, \frac{dy}{dx}\right) = b,$$

give rise to the same differential equation of the second order, shew how the general solution of an equation of the form

$$F\left\{\phi\left(x, y, \frac{dy}{dx}\right), \psi\left(x, y, \frac{dy}{dx}\right)\right\} = 0,$$

may be found without integration.

Apply this or any other method to the discovery of the general solution of the equation

$$x^3 y \left(\frac{dy}{dx}\right)^2 + (a^4 - 2x^2 y^2) \frac{dy}{dx} + xy^3 = 0.$$

6. Enunciate and explain d'Alembert's principle. Apply it to determine the small oscillations in space of a uniform heavy rod of length $2a$, suspended from a fixed point by an inextensible string of length l fastened to one extremity. Prove that, if x be one of the horizontal co-ordinates of that extremity of the rod to which the string is fastened,

$$x = A \sin(n_1 t + a) + B \sin(n_2 t + \beta),$$

where n_1, n_2 are the two positive roots of the equation,

$$aln^4 - (4a + 3l) gn^2 + 3g^2 = 0,$$

and A, B, a, β, are arbitrary constants.

vii. A rigid body is rotating about an axis through its centre of gravity, when a certain point of the body becomes suddenly fixed, the axis being simultaneously set free; find the equations of the new instantaneous axis; and prove that, if it be parallel to the originally fixed axis, the point must lie in the line represented by the equations,

$$a^2 lx + b^2 my + c^2 nz = 0,$$

$$(b^2 - c^2)\frac{x}{l} + (c^2 - a^2)\frac{y}{m} + (a^2 - b^2)\frac{z}{n} = 0;$$

the principal axes through the centre of gravity being taken as axes of co-ordinates, a, b, c the radii of gyration about these lines, and l, m, n the direction-cosines of the originally fixed axis referred to them.

8. Explain the physical meaning of the term
$$\frac{15}{8} mea \cos\{(2 - 2m - c)\theta - 2\beta + a\}$$
in the expression for the reciprocal of the Moon's radius vector.

Calculate roughly the proportionate alteration in the Moon's mean distance produced by this term, and its period. Why is this term usually taken in combination with the elliptic inequality?

ix. Prove the following relation between the perturbations of a planet in longitude and radius vector
$$\delta\theta = \frac{1}{h}\left\{\frac{d(2r\delta r)}{dt} - \frac{1}{r}\frac{dr}{dt}r\delta r + 3\iint\frac{d(R)}{dt}dt^2 + 2\int r\frac{dR}{dr}\,dt\right\},$$
h being twice the sectorial area described in a unit of time by the undisturbed planet round the Sun; and find the corresponding relation whatever be the law of force, provided it be central and a function of the distance only, and provided such a function as R can be found.

10. If the object-glass of a telescope be covered over by a diaphragm, pierced in the centre by a small hole, the form of which is a rectangle, state generally the nature of the spectra formed about the image of a star on a screen placed at the focus.

If the hole be circular and the screen be pushed towards the lens, prove that, when the light is homogeneous, the centre is alternately bright and dark. Trace also the order of the colours seen if the light be not homogeneous.

FRIDAY, *Jan.* 20. 9 *to* 12.

1. When the reciprocal of a circle is taken with respect to another circle, investigate the nature of the reciprocal conic, and the polars of its centre and further focus.

OA, OB are common tangents to two conics having a common focus S, CA, CB are tangents at one of their points of intersection, BD, AE tangents intersecting CA, CB in D, E. Prove that SDE is a straight line.

O

ii. Define the term potential of a mass, the particles of which attract according to the law of nature; and prove that, if a body moveable about a fixed axis be subject to the action of an attracting mass of which the potential is V, then $\iiint \frac{dV}{d\theta} dm$ is the moment which must be impressed upon the body about that axis in order to produce equilibrium, where θ is the inclination of the plane through the fixed axis and the particle of which the mass is dm to a fixed plane.

A uniform straight line, the particles of which attract according to this law, acts upon a rigid uniform circular arc in the same plane with the line, of which the radius is equal to the line, and which is moveable about an axis through its centre perpendicular to its plane, the axis being coincident with one extremity of the line. Prove that the moment necessary to produce equilibrium when the bounding radii are inclined at the angles a and β to the line produced is proportional to

$$\log \frac{\sec \frac{a}{2} + 1}{\sec \frac{\beta}{2} + 1}.$$

3. Define lines of curvature on a surface; and find their differential equation. Prove that one line of curvature at any point very near an umbilicus passes through that umbilicus.

4. State and prove the principle of Vis Viva. If an elastic string, whose natural length is that of a uniform rod, be attached to the rod at both ends and suspended by the middle point, prove by means of Vis Viva that the rod will sink until the strings are inclined to the horizon at an angle θ, which satisfies the equation

$$\cot^3 \frac{\theta}{2} - \cot \frac{\theta}{2} - 2n = 0,$$

where the tension of the string, when stretched to double its length is n times the weight.

If the string be suspended by a point, not in the middle, write down the equation of Vis Viva.

v. If a spheroid of revolution be moveable about its centre which is fixed, and θ be the inclination of its equator to a fixed plane,

ψ the inclination of the line of intersection of its equator with this plane to a fixed line in the plane, A and C the respective moments of inertia about the axis of figure and a line in the equator respectively, L and M the moments of impressed couples about the line of intersection of the equator with the fixed plane, and a line in the equator perpendicular to this latter line respectively, ω the angular velocity about the axis of figure, prove that

$$C\frac{d^2\theta}{dt^2} - C\left(\frac{d\psi}{dt}\right)^2 \sin\theta\cos\theta + A\omega\sin\theta\frac{d\psi}{dt} = L,$$

$$C\frac{d}{dt}\left(\frac{d\psi}{dt}\sin\theta\right) + C\frac{d\psi}{dt}\frac{d\theta}{dt}\cos\theta - A\omega\frac{d\theta}{dt} = M,$$

hence deduce the precessional and nutational velocity of the Earth's axis, assuming the effect of the Sun's action to be a couple of which the moment is $m\sin\Delta\cos\Delta$ about an axis in the equator 90° distant from the Sun, m being a very small quantity, A and C very nearly equal, and the Sun's motion in declination and right-ascension being neglected.

vi. If μ be a given function of the co-ordinates x and y of any point in a plane curve, prove that if the curve be so determined as to render the integral $\int\mu ds$ between given limits a maximum or minimum, then

$$\frac{1}{\rho} = -\frac{1}{\mu}\left(\frac{d\mu}{dx}\cos\alpha + \frac{d\mu}{dy}\cos\beta\right),$$

ρ being the radius of curvature at any point, and α, β the acute angles which the normal at that point makes with the axes of x and y respectively.

If a solid of revolution be immersed in a heavy homogeneous fluid with its axis vertical, prove that, when the total normal pressure on the surface is a minimum, its form must be such that the numerical value of the diameter of curvature of the meridian at any point is a harmonic mean between the segments of the normal to the surface at that point intercepted between the point and the surface of the fluid and between the point and the axis, respectively.

7. Supposing the orbits of a disturbing and disturbed planet to be in the same plane, prove that the rate of change of the

longitude of perihelion of the instantaneous ellipse of the disturbed planet is

$$\frac{n_1 a_1 (1-e_1^2)^{\frac{1}{2}}}{\mu e_1} \frac{dR}{de_1}.$$

In what respects do the theories of the motion of the apsides in lunar and planetary disturbances present themselves respectively in simpler aspects?

viii. Explain the phenomenon of external conical refraction where a small pencil of light passes through a biaxal crystal; and describe an experiment by which this phenomenon may be manifested.

If the crystal be bounded by planes perpendicular to the line bisecting the acute angles between the optic axes, write down equations whence the equation of the cone of emerging rays may be obtained.

FRIDAY, $Jan.$ 20. $1\frac{1}{2}$ to 4.

1. IF a, β, γ be the respective distances of a straight line from the three angular points of a triangle ABC, these distances being reckoned positive or negative according as their directions fall within the angles of the triangle itself or their supplements, investigate the following relation,

$(a \sin A)^2 + (\beta \sin B)^2 + (\gamma \sin C)^2 - 2 \cos A \sin B \sin C \beta\gamma - 2 \cos B$

$\sin C \sin A \gamma a - 2 \cos C \sin A \sin B a\beta = 4R^2 \sin^2 A \sin^2 B \sin^2 C$,

where R is the radius of the circumscribed circle.

2. State the positive and negative characteristics of a singular solution of a differential equation; and shew how it is deduced from the complete primitive. Shew also how the singular solution of a differential equation of the first order is obtained from the equation itself.

Obtain the singular solution of the equation of which

$$y \cos^2 m = 2 \cos (x - 2m)$$

is the complete primitive; and find the singular solution of the equation

$$(x+y)^2 \left(\frac{dy}{dx}\right)^2 - (x^2 - y^2) \left(\frac{dy}{dx}\right)^2 + 1 = 0.$$

iii. Prove that, in any curve of double curvature, the locus of the centres of spherical curvature is the edge of regression of the envelope of the normal planes. Prove also that this locus cannot be an evolute.

The normal plane to the locus of the centres of circular curvature bisects the radius of spherical curvature.

4. Determine the class of curves which possess the property that the locus of the extremity of the polar subtangent of any one is similar to the curve itself.

Shew that $r\theta \epsilon^{m\theta} = a$ is the equation of such a curve.

v. Investigate the general equations of motion of a sphere under the action of any forces.

If a homogeneous sphere roll on a perfectly rough plane under the action of any forces whatever, of which the resultant passes through the centre of the sphere, the motion of the centre of gravity will be the same as if the plane were smooth and all the forces were reduced in a certain constant ratio; and the plane is the only surface which possesses this property.

6. Assuming the following equations for the rate of variation of the inclination and of the longitude of the line of nodes of a planet m disturbed by a planet m',

$$\frac{d\Omega}{dt} = \frac{na}{\mu(1-e^2)^{\frac{1}{2}} \sin i} \frac{dR}{di},$$

$$\frac{di}{dt} = -\frac{na}{\mu(1-e^2)^{\frac{1}{2}}} \left\{ \frac{1}{\sin i} \frac{dR}{d\Omega} + \tan \frac{i}{2} \left(\frac{dR}{d\epsilon} + \frac{dR}{d\varpi} \right) \right\},$$

investigate general expressions for i and Ω, so far as they are affected by the effect of the following terms in the expansion of R,

$$-m' \left[2D_1 ee' \cos(\varpi' - \varpi) + \tfrac{1}{8} aa' D_1 \left\{ \tan^2 i - 2 \tan i \tan i' \cos(\Omega - \Omega') \right\} \right].$$

vii. Prove that, if the Earth be considered as a homogeneous mass of fluid in the form of a spheroid, revolving with a uniform angular velocity about its axis, gravity at any point acts along the normal, and is proportional to the part of the normal intercepted between the point of contact and the plane of the equator.

If the Earth be completely covered by a sea of small depth, prove that the depth in latitude l is very nearly equal to $H(1 - \epsilon \sin^2 l)$ where H is the depth at the equator, and ϵ the ellipticity of the Earth.

8. A thin plate of Iceland spar, cut perpendicularly to its axis, is interposed between two tourmalines, used as a polarizing and analyzing plate, and a pencil of parallel rays is transmitted through the crystals. Assuming that the difference of retardation of the ordinary and extraordinary rays, when a ray is transmitted through a plate of Iceland spar in a direction inclined to its axis at a small angle i varies as $T \sin^2 i$, investigate an expression for the illumination at any point of the field of view, the axes of the tourmalines being parallel; and hence deduce a description of the phenomena observed, supposing the light (1) to be homogeneous, (2) to be white.

ix. State under what circumstances in the motion of a fluid we may assume $udx + vdy + wdz$ to be a perfect differential of some function.

Assuming this function to be ϕ, and the fluid to be homogeneous, investigate the equation

$$\frac{d^2\phi}{dx^2} + \frac{d^2\phi}{dy^2} + \frac{d^2\phi}{dz^2} = 0.$$

The base of an infinite cylinder is the space contained between an equilateral hyperbola and its asymptotes. A plane is drawn perpendicular to the base, and cutting it in a straight line parallel to an asymptote, and the portion of the cylinder between this plane and its parallel asymptote is filled with homogeneous fluid, under the action of no impressed forces. The plane being suddenly removed, determine the motion; and prove that the free surface of the fluid will remain plane, and advance with a uniform velocity proportional to $\sqrt{\varpi}$, where ϖ is the pressure at an infinite distance, which is supposed to remain constant throughout the motion.

www.ingramcontent.com/pod-product-compliance
Lightning Source LLC
Chambersburg PA
CBHW020918230426
43666CB00008B/1489